Illustrated
LOTUS
BUYER'S
GUIDE ™

Illustrated
LOTUS
BUYER'S GUIDE™

Graham Arnold

Motorbooks International
Publishers & Wholesalers Inc
Osceola, Wisconsin 54020, USA ®

First published in 1986 by Motorbooks International Publishers & Wholesalers Inc, PO Box 2, 729 Prospect Avenue, Osceola, WI 54020 USA

© Graham Arnold, 1986

All rights reserved. With the exception of quoting brief passages for the purposes of review no part of this publication may be reproduced without prior written permission from the publisher

Motorbooks International is a certified trademark, registered with the United States Patent Office

Printed and bound in the United States of America

The information in this book is true and complete to the best of our knowledge. All recommendations are made without any guarantee on the part of the author or publisher, who also disclaim any liability incurred in connection with the use of this data or specific details

Library of Congress Cataloging-in-Publication Data
Arnold, Graham
  Illustrated Lotus buyer's guide.
    1. Lotus automobile. 2. Automobiles—Purchasing.
I. Title.
TL215.L67A75 1986 629.2′222   86-12771
ISBN 0-87938-217-1 (pbk.)

Cover photography by Andrew Morland

Motorbooks International books are also available at discounts in bulk quantity for industrial or sales-promotional use. For details write to Special Sales Manager at the Publisher's address

Contents

	An appreciation — Colin Chapman, genius	7
	What is Lotus?	10
	Choosing the cars for this book	15
	How to buy a Lotus	23
1	Six and Seven	26
2	Eleven	45
3	Elite (Climax)	52
4	Elan	62
5	Ford Cortina Lotus	76
6	Elan Plus 2	85
7	Europa	92
8	Elite and Eclat (Sprint)	103
9	Esprit	115
10	Chrysler/Talbot Sunbeam	126
	Lotus in the United States	132
	Restoration tips	134
	Lotus/Ford twincam	144

Appendix

Racing road cars	151
Non-factory cars	152
Replicas, look-alikes and forgeries	153
The Cortina Lotus and Sunbeam Lotus in rallies	154
Clubs	155
Sources	158

An appreciation—Colin Chapman, genius

I had the privilege of working with Colin Chapman as one of his "lieutenants" through two of the possibly most exciting periods in the firm's history. The period from 1963 to 1971 was tough enough, but my return to the fold from 1977 to 1981 proved to be even more challenging and diverse. Innes Ireland, in *Road & Track*, wrote after Chapman's death, "And so Colin had the quality to bring out the best from people by his example and persuasion. Equally he had the ability to crush and extinguish the fire that he had kindled when that person served their purpose, or when there was a better prospect on the horizon."

Chapman as an innovator was without equal in the auto industry. Chapman as a motivator was a tyrant, but when he wanted

Colin Chapman, the businessman. Official corporate photograph in 1982.

Colin Chapman, founding genius of Lotus, at a grand prix in 1982. He died in December of that year.

something he was an absolute charmer—especially if money was involved. His greatest fascination (and an indication to his inner character) involved his hatred of rules. Rules were there to be circumvented, they were a challenge. Consequently, the story of his life is filled with examples of how he battled the rule makers and frequently won. In motor racing he was always one step ahead. (He even rewrote the "rules of accountancy" at

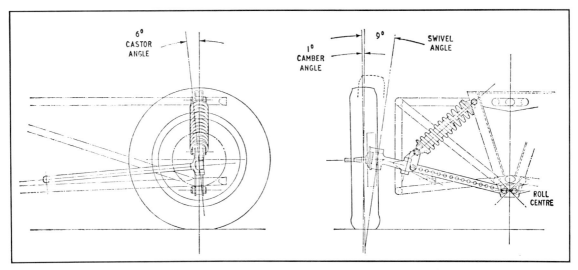

Divided Ford beam axle, a la Lotus Mark 8, ably illustrates Chapman's desire for simplicity and lightness.

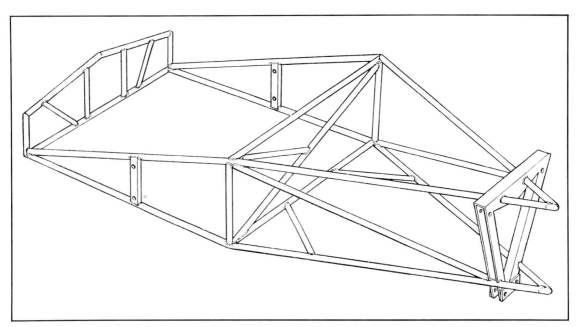

Bare chassis of the Mark 8, which together with a stressed undertray and body panels, completed a strong, rigid structure. Chapman genius at work.

one important stage when a rule stood between him and his first million.) His devious approach to rules and regulations saw his innovations banned on a regular basis and he developed a passionate hatred of governments that introduced legislation intended to constrain designers of new automobiles and new automotive concepts. In desperation, he even turned to the "clean sheet of paper" world of luxury yacht design.

We had many intense arguments, but in retrospect I won some that really mattered concerning product policy (especially on the Elan, Europa and Elan Plus 2) by having my facts ready and refusing to give in to a lot of shouting and clenched white knuckles. We weren't friends but we respected each other's abilities. I admired him for his decisiveness—he sacked me when sales slumped in 1970 and I was punch-drunk with frustrations.

Chapman can never be replaced by one person in racing car and road car design; perhaps those times are past. In retrospect he was totally wasted messing about with automobiles, much as we all love them. He should have been working on a greater scale, as he had the genius to rival Von Braun in aerospace or design a better aircraft than the Concorde. But what luck for Lotus lovers!

The death of Colin Chapman marked the end of an era. The letters that go to make up the name Lotus will appear on many cars in the future, but only time will tell if some new genius emerges to carry on his good work on road and track. The cars were of the Lotus marque but those initials on the badge were ACBC—Anthony Colin Bruce Chapman.

Graham Arnold
Norfolk, England

Spot the Lotus models! The Cherry Hill, New Jersey, gathering was the first for Lotus Ltd in 1981, where there appeared more Europas than any other model. Lotus Ltd, Maryland

What is Lotus?

Remember the Bible story of David and Goliath? David took this very aerodynamic, lightweight rock and struck Goliath between the eyes on his first try. By the same token, Lotus cars will outrun vehicles costing twice the price with twice the power. They will do this while giving double pleasure to the driver as he takes the opposition deeper into corners than the other driver's brakes can accommodate. Then he pours on the power in mid-turn to open up a massive gap in just a few seconds of superlative handling. I can remember out-dragging several big-engined hot rods with an Elan Special Equipment in 1968. When they asked how big the motor was, they would not believe it was only 1600 cc.

When prospective Lotus importers came

The original Lotus factory at Hornsey, North London, much as it is today. Club Lotus England

to the factory to discuss selling Chapman's cars, several were literally thrown out—megabuck checkbooks and all—when they said "Ship us the cars less engine and gearbox because we plan to put in some real American muscle, you know, a V-8 like the Shelby Cobras."

Chapman design philosophy and attitude

In the early days of Lotus, Chapman was moonlighting from his senior position as a stress engineer with the British Aluminium Company. He was heavily involved in lightweight structures. This, combined with his love of aircraft (the ultimate lightweight structure), made him think of cars as too heavy and therefore slow to accelerate, harder to stop and more difficult to manage in turns. He also realized that the 75 bhp engine in a 750 pound car would beat a car with a 100 bhp engine weighing 1,000 pounds, all other things being equal. Chapman looked at the state-of-the-art and resolved to jump at least two steps ahead. (He invented the quantum leap, even if some of his steps took him outside the boundaries into the swamp!) As he turned tradition on its ear almost every day, he was resented by the establishment, which soon changed the rules to retain the status quo and fend off the challenge from this young upstart.

Chapman designed an ultralight rigid chassis, fitted a suspension that featured a long movement which was soft and progressively damped. He added a wind-cheating bodyshell that was as light and as aerodynamic as the contemporary state-of-the-art would allow. He put in an engine that was also light and compact but that gave "adequate power." He was not forever screaming at the engine man for more power. "I don't ask for all the problems provided by extra power until I have tuned the chassis and the aerodynamics to the ultimate," he once said, "and then before I talk to the engine man I suggest to the *driver* that *we* might be able to find somebody able to go faster!"

The Lotus factory today.

In his later designs he focused on maintaining the same "attitude," whether the car was accelerating, cornering or braking hard. Once he had achieved a totally constant body attitude he could turn to ground-effect aerodynamics, knowing that the effect would not be lost at any vital moment. He was a master of rigidity with lightness, aerodynamics and soft suspension with wheels that remained upright. In his later years, he became an international expert on exotic high-strength lightweight materials. His designs were elegant, very simple and yet full of innovative genius.

Chapman kept one of every current Lotus car made in his private stable. He drove them fast and hard but when he wanted to drive long distances he could be seen, initially, behind the wheel of his 3.8 liter Jaguar sedan, then a series of sumptuous Mercedes-Benz sedans or the Ford Galaxie from Indianapolis.

On PR occasions he was seen in a Ford Zodiac Executive loaned to him (at my suggestion) by Ford of Britain. However, any distance over sixty miles would be covered in one of his personal or company aircraft. These progressed from a Piper Cherokee-6 to a Twin Commanche to a Piper Navajo Chieftain (turbocharged and pressurized model) to a Cessna Jet and a Bell Jet Ranger helicopter (with Essex sponsorship money).

Chapman's use of aircraft and interest in them created a continuous input of information on the use of exotic materials, turbocharging and so on. He drove Lotus cars flat out and stormed into the company's development section "spitting blood" if he found something not to his liking. He did not want to meet owners in case they complained, for he maintained the attitude of a racing car manufacturer toward his touring car customers: "Of course they break—that's all part of Lotus ownership."

Once he approved a design, he could not wait for the glory and publicity of announcement day, followed (we hoped) by rave reviews. The Europa S1 made its debut with fixed windows because he would not wait for the wind-down variety to be developed. Chapman's impatience was the main motivating force throughout the company and one of his greatest qualities. When he died, the pace of Lotus died with him, at least for a year. In fact, many people breathed a sigh of relief, as he was a cruel taskmaster to those who were late with vital programs.

It is not true that he saw his cars just as a source of profit. He loved every one at the time of its conception and birth—but not for

A happy work team at Lotus about to complete the 25,000th engine, a US-specification unit for an Esprit.

The author (right) discusses a point with Colin Chapman during a visit by Members of Parliament. Club Lotus England

long. He was always getting ready for the next one.

Chapman ethics

I must now recall an incident from my many years as director of Lotus to explain one important factor. Chapman and I were discussing his public image objectives for 1970 and how he wanted to be viewed by the world (especially since I was trying to get his name changed to Sir Colin Chapman). He said, "I want to be seen as Britain's Mr. Porsche." I said that was impossible and he frowned and asked why.

"Because you're a crook," I replied starring back at him. He half smiled and asked why I felt that way.

"Right, Ferdinand Porsche is approached by two of his engineers with wheel bearings for a new car. Porsche says, 'What is their expected road life?' And the engineers reveal that one costing $15 will last three years and another costing $30 will run about five years. 'Find me a bearing that will last ten years,' he dictates."

"So?" asked Chapman.

I continued, "Two engineers come to you with two possible bearings. One will cost $5 and last one year and the other will cost $7 and last two years. You ask, 'How long is our warranty?'"

Chapman smiled because he knew I was right.

When asked about his race cars as compared with Ferrari, considering they were about equal as far as Grand Prix victories, Chapman said, "I design them light and possibly fragile, and beef them up till they stay in one piece long enough for Jimmy (Clark) to win. Now Ferrari, he makes them too heavy and takes weight out till they win—or break."

Lotus cars were designed to make the biggest profit possible. The formula was quite simple: He took the materials and labor and multiplied them by a factor of 2.8 (which eventually increased to 3) to get the UK retail price. Cutting the material or component costs without reducing the retail price gave good, extra profits. For example, I discovered that Ford had produced a semi-close-ratio gearbox for its Corsair 2000 in 1964. This, with the 3.7:1 differential, could be bought to save $75 per car or return us an extra profit.

Similar savings were used to stave off price increases. We acquired as many parts as possible from other manufacturers' parts bins, and frequently found their van parts costing less than car parts.

Almost every year the company organized a campaign to "take pounds out of the cars." Of course, we were talking about both pounds in weight and pounds sterling! In one instance I was invited to test drive, over a long weekend, the definitive incorporation of all suggestions. The car didn't last past Friday evening, as its first test was to get from the factory to the local pub in less than two minutes. To break the magical two minutes one had to lock up the brakes and slide into the first entrance. As I attempted this, I developed a very long pedal travel as the complete brake assembly disappeared through the much thinner firewall into the engine bay. The car was twenty pounds lighter, partially via the reduction in firewall fiberglass thickness! Needless to say we didn't adopt *all* the ideas incorporated in that animal.

One of our favorite money-saving ideas was to push the frontiers of other manufacturers' "overengineering," which meant a part built for a smaller car would be tested in a Lotus to see if it was sufficiently over-engineered and understressed to give adequate life.

The ultimate example was Chapman's use of the constant velocity joints used in an

Lotus Mk III in 1953. More than 30 years ago this was quick enough. The race organizers were already rewriting the rules to restrain Chapman.

unloved British car called the Austin 1800. It had a transverse 1800 cc engine producing 95 bhp. Colin fit them to the Lotus 49 Grand Prix cars where they absorbed up to 350 bhp for a whole race and most of the cooling lap. We also got very near the limit on road car radiator size. They got smaller and cheaper as the years went by and Chapman knew what he was doing.

In the South African Grand Prix, other cars had large air inlets to their radiators, and ducts chopped everywhere to get the heat out. The Team Lotus cars were shipped with fifty percent bigger radiators. "Engines in good condition don't overheat," he said. Manufacturers undercool them by ignorance or design.

In some cases we did not follow this policy, especially with brakes and heaters, because Chapman liked to keep warm while sitting still. So we took the heaters from big cars and brakes from fast cars that weighed fifty percent more than a Lotus.

As you can see, many Lotus parts are common to other European contemporaries but not all were exported to the United States. So don't go looking in the local junkyard for a Commer Cob van to find new door handles for your Elan S2.

Lotus Formula One car stripped of its bodywork. Chapman led a team of designers, engineers, chemists and craftsmen with state-of-the-art creations. He, and they, had come a long, long way in 30 odd years. Club Lotus England

Choosing the cars for this book

The cars I have chosen come from the Lotus road car line and are either highly valuable or great fun to drive—frequently, they are both. The amount written about each car reflects two criteria: a lot means they are fun and collectible, a little means you draw your own conclusions. Pure race cars, where covered, get a minimum of my pen-time as very few readers will actually buy this book with the idea of finding, restoring and then racing a classic Lotus car.

Lotus was a marvelously disjointed company that lurched from success to crisis, windfall profit to sudden deep depression. There was a basic overall plan that was adjusted to suit circumstances. Chapman once said, "We planned a three-model lineup consisting of the Elite, Eclat (Sprint) and

A typical Club Lotus regional meet in Great Britain, at Castle Combe. Take your pick. Club Lotus England

the Esprit." All but the former came about by accident or market/dealer pressures.

People ask, "Was the Lotus Six to be called a Lotus Six or a Lotus 6?" and "Was the Elan Plus Two, the Plus 2, the 2+2 or the Two Plus Two?" As the man responsible for preparing the sale literature at that time, I can reply "yes" to all of the questions.

We were making and selling a lot of fun cars, not making rules and giving purists and nit-pickers years of excitement as they try to write books like this. No doubt every chassis and part number of a Bugatti is written down in some big, dust-covered book, probably in immaculate handwriting. At Lotus we lost the books, couldn't remember what the last chassis number was, left out a few, duplicated a few others, went back to where we started, changed the system a dozen times and even enjoyed thinking of all the confusion we created. (However, I have stuck to consistent names and numbers in this book.)

Cars were named over a few pints of beer, providing the name started with "E." (And, of course, the tax man had the devil's own problems trying to work out how many cars had been made, who had them and for how much. It was once said that the Inland Revenue Service threatened any young officer with "a year on the Lotus account" if he stepped out of line. That was enough!)

Why start with "E"? When Lotus got to the Eleven, Chapman liked the way the words Lotus Eleven rolled off the tongue; so for no other reason, he decreed that all Lotus cars would, in the future, have names starting with "E"—but only if they were road cars made purely by Lotus. One day the names will run out. There were some who thought Lotus had plumbed the depths with Eclat, until it came up with Etna (the name of a well-known volcano) to replace the fire-prone Esprit. We spent many a happy hour with English and foreign dictionaries looking at names; the Europa was eventually not called the "Elfin" because that means the end in another language!

I tried to stop it all by calling the Eclat replacement the XL but Lotus used Excel. I mean to say X begins with an "E," doesn't it?

Here are the cars with their ratings:

	Fun	Investment	Anguish
Lotus Six	8	10	3
Lotus Seven	8	10	3
Lotus Eleven	7	10	6
Lotus Elite (Climax)	6	10	6
Lotus Elan	7	6	6
Lotus Elan Sprint Drop Head	8	9	3
Ford Cortina Lotus	5	7	3
Lotus Elan Plus 2	6	5	5
Lotus Europa (Renault)	5	5	8
Lotus Europa Twincam	8	8	6
Lotus Elite and Eclat (Sprint)	6	4	9
Lotus Esprit S1 and S2	6	5	9
Lotus Esprit S3 and Turbo	8	7	5
Chrysler/Talbot Sunbeam Lotus	8	6	4

The anguish factor reflects two aspects of ownership: first, the likelihood of outright failure and frequency of nagging faults; and second, the shortage of spare parts and/or information, even sympathy.

For example, a Europa (Renault) has a high anguish factor because, as any long-suffering owner will tell you, there is a constant search for parts: doors fall off, chassis droop, irreplaceable windshield trims disappear and so on. Not to mention that you will not get back home under your own steam from any journey over 100 miles when it is important to do so. Threaten to drive your car to the junk yard and it will cruise all day at 100 mph and outhandle any Porsche that comes your way!

Which are the most collectible Lotus cars? This is much like trying to decide which wine to put in the cellar. If at the end of the day you plan to enjoy the flavor, your choice may be different from the person who wants to see the biggest possible appreciation. So, do you want to enjoy the dual pleasure of driving your car and soaking up its beauty or do you plan to sell your collection in ten years' time to pay for a cruise to Tahiti? With this in mind, my first list below is aesthetic and the second (tongue in cheek) is financial.

Lotus Lover's Collection
1. 1958 Lotus Eleven Le Mans Climax
2. 1962 Lotus Elite Climax Super 95 (ZF)
3. 1967 Lotus Elan Special Equipment S3 Drop Head
4. 1969 Lotus Seven Twincam

Capitalist's Collection
1. 1951 Lotus Mk 3
2. 1958 Lotus Eleven Le Mans Climax, Monza record car
3. 1962 Lotus Elite Climax Super 95 (ZF)
4. 1971 Lotus Elan Sprint Drop Head in red, white and gold

In the Lotus Lover's Collection I have listed cars that can be purchased on the open market to give an inordinate amount of pleasure to the owner and driver. The Capitalist's Collection is almost a duplicate but I have been more specific. For example, there is only one original Mk 3 and that is *not* for sale. If it was, Hazel Chapman (Colin's widow) would outbid even the Getty Trust to get it back. Then I have listed the actual Lotus Eleven with faired-in, bubble-top cockpit used by Stirling Moss at Monza to attack a series of speed records in 1957. That car is still in existence but not known to be for sale. Then I have the Elan Big Valve Sprint with its distinctive John Player Gold Leaf (cigarettes) color scheme. These four cars should be in a museum where they would appreciate faster and give better return on capital. But the Lotus Lover's Collection should be out there on the road and track being driven.

Anyone who runs figures through a computer playing "spot the investment" will not hit on classic Lotus cars as an untapped possibility for making a million or achieving earnings ahead of the market. A well-restored Lotus is a hedge against inflation, and a whole lot of fun. To extract the maximum benefit from owning a classic Lotus, the collector needs a commitment to the marque, good premises, adequate finances and enough knowledge to avoid being cheated.

It is hoped that devoted restorers and collectors of Lotus cars will not attempt to build up massive closed collections hidden away from the public. As president of the Lotus Heritage movement, I hope that the maximum number of cars will be held by the largest possible number of owners and that these owners will actually take them out and drive them regularly.

Worldwide, good examples of the marque appreciate ahead of inflation, but investment in the car to save it from the wreckers or to improve its quality will more than wipe out the appreciation potential for the next few years. If, for example, you buy an Elan as a "basket case" for $2,000, it will require an investment of at least $8,000 to make it worth entering the concours at a classic car meet. The winner will have invested $15,000. You will be hard pressed to get $10,000 for the car and the winner can whistle into the wind all day if he expects $17,000-20,000.

Where, oh where, do I find a Lotus?

Literally thousands of Lotus cars have gone out of circulation in the United States for three reasons. The first is ignorance. This funny, plastic imported car has been lying around somebody's backyard and no one seems interested in what it is, what it is worth, or in getting rid of it. In your wildest dreams you just happen by and say to yourself, "That's one of the ex-works Sebring Elites," and to the owner you say, "I'll take that ugly handbuilt pile of junk off your hands for $50." Such finds are indeed out there but happening upon them is like panning for gold—and potentially just as rewarding.

To find a Lotus, scan the advertisements in *Road & Track, Car and Driver, Autoweek, Hemmings Motor News* and the Sunday edition of *The New York Times*. There are also many excellent magazines and bulletins put out by the various Lotus clubs in the United States and Europe. To help things along, place want ads in appropriate publications.

The second reason for these lost Lotus cars is procrastination: "I'm going to restore every last nut and bolt in that car when the kids grow up—in fact, they can help!"

Reason number three is avarice. "Yes, sorry, but somebody with green eyes got to that car first and now it's in his collection until his eventual widow sells it and moves to Miami."

The best source of a used Lotus is among the procrastinators. They know in their hearts that they will not finish the restoration. One Lotus owner's wife in this group summed it up perfectly: "He swears he is going to fix that Europa some day." The restoration never gets off the ground and suddenly the space is needed for a pool or patio extension or Junior's first car. So if you can, get behind the left shoulder of a few procrastinating types and whisper, "Dollars today for your car; I'll restore it and you can have the first drive."

For Europe, read Britain because Lotus Cars never made many sales to the Europeans, yet now they have become cult collector items in Germany and Holland. The remaining left-hand-drive European-specification cars are nearly all priced well above the American market and usually *not* for sale. There is also a slight moral barrier against selling European classics to the United States or Japan; in fact, I'm told, one Lotus club will throw you out if you sell your Lotus outside Britain!

There are many good, used Lotus cars advertised in British magazines such as *Exchange & Mart*, *Autosport*, *Motor Sport*, *Thoroughbred & Classic Car*, *Classic & Sports Car* and *Motoring News*. It must be understood that "ripping off the Yanks" is a European pastime dating back to the immediate postwar days, when the first 250 pound tourists arrived with cameras bouncing off their bellies, large cigars and billfolds full of dollars. The motor trade still has its horse-trading reputation, so buy a used Lotus in Europe through a trustworthy European or a Lotus club official.

There are US regulations which some say can be circumvented by very expensive "shops" or semilegal paperwork on post-1967 cars. Check very carefully before you import.

Currently, the pound versus dollar relationship is still running slightly in favor of Americans spending dollars in Britain, and everyone knows it! However, very restorable, classic Lotus cars can be purchased in Britain, albeit in right-hand-drive form, and much of the restoration work can be carried out prior to shipment. A genuine Lotus chassis frame or Spyder alternative space-frame will cost a lot less to purchase and have fitted in Britain than it would in the United States. The same applies to major engine and transmission overhauls, suspension rebuilds and so on. As an added bonus a greater percentage of the parts will be genuine Lotus parts bought directly from the factory if you use a listed specialist or a Lotus restoration agent.

American paint jobs are usually better than British ones, so let the dockers or air freighters mess up the old paint (you can claim "in transit damage" on the insurance and get a contribution toward a new paint job). As mentioned earlier, check with your federal and state government agencies for the legal requirements to bring a British car into the United States for use on the roads.

Lotus types

When Dennis Ortenberger subtitled his excellent book on the Lotus Elite "The Racing Car for the Road" he pinpointed a delicate area. The Elite was never conceived as a racing car and for a while, during its currency, Chapman was upset at the idea it might be raced. Then he set about producing look-alike racing versions to meet demand and scoop up many fine victories that were just waiting for a car that fit the needs of Le Mans, Sebring and others.

In the case of the Elan type 26, Chapman issued orders that it was *not* to be homologated for international competition. So I homologated it through Switzerland, secretly, to meet the demands of European dealers whose national motor clubs wouldn't let a car into a village slalom without full FIA (Federal International des Automobiles) recognition and homologation certification.

In the early days most Lotus cars were designed to be driven to the circuit, raced and then driven home. However, many an owner came home on the train with his trophy in a paper bag and the wreckage following on a transporter. This design trend did not include the Type 14 already mentioned and died out with the Type 23 on. From there we had Lotus cars in three categories: pure racing cars, used team cars and road cars.

The pure racing cars were manufactured by Lotus Engineering, then Lotus Components Limited, later called Lotus Racing, and carried a chassis tag declaring the manufacturer's name as such.

The team usually sold its cars too late. By that I mean that at the end of the last race of the season it could command a much higher price than by mid-season the next year when the latest models had rendered them obsolete. But Chapman hung on to the old cars in case the new cars didn't function straight out of the box. In fact, the 72s were dusted off "for just one more season" so often that they went from the world's greatest F1 cars to the biggest joke in five seasons. In some cases former team cars were sold and then reappeared under new names (the first Brabham F1 cars were actually reworked Lotus models). After Indianapolis each year, one or more of the cars were sold. One car, sold to Dan Gurney, is reputed to have won as an Eagle!

Although Chapman declared that no road car was to be raced, he recognized the publicity value of look-alike racing versions, starting with the Elite type 14. Then the racing Elan 26R shared a good deal of the silhouette, chassis and power unit/drivetrain with the touring car. The factory Cortina Lotus also looked like a road car but had ultrathin body panels and reworked suspension.

The Type 47 Europa came along because a major sponsor wanted to have its brand name seen, not just at F1 level but also in clubman class race success. So the red, white and gold of John Player Gold Leaf cigarettes appeared on the 47s. When the cars were upgraded to accommodate the Lotus two-liter and sprouted a variety of unrecognizable aerodynamic devices, the Europa tag was dropped and they were called Lotus 62s.

No official racing version of any production Lotus car was made after the Europa, although some lightweight Esprit bodyshells were sold "GM style, through the back door" to teams that did nothing notable with them.

Lotus enthusiasts could be excused for getting excited by so-called Esprits in a European silhouette class of sports car racing. These are simply Esprit replica bodyshells on something like a single-seater BMW-powered March Formula 2 chassis and raced as a Lotus Esprit. Today, Lotus frowns openly on anyone who seeks to compete in a modified-production Lotus, following Chapman's tradition that one had to go back to the drawing board to produce something that looked like a road car but went like a race winner.

Up to and including the Lotus Eleven, all cars were known as Mk 1, Mk 2 and so on, but then became Type 12 and so forth. The following listing will be helpful in differentiating them.

Mark 1 An Austin 7-based trials car used in off-the-road events. The first car to carry the name Lotus. Location unknown. 1948.

Mark 2 Really a Mark IA, as it incorporated many improvements and had a Ford side-valve engine. Used in one or two races by Chapman. 1949-50.

Mark 3 The first Lotus to annoy the establishment; Chapman's clever engine modifications were subsequently banned. Still based on a 1930 Austin 7 and raced in the class known as the 750 Formula, a series for Austin 7-based cars. This and the Mk 3B are still in collectors' hands. 1951, only two built, plus one spare chassis.

Mark 4 The first product of Lotus Engineering Limited and another Ford 1172 cc side-valve-powered trials car. 1952, one only.

Mark 5 This project was never started but was intended to be a 100 mph 750 cc racer.

Mark 6 Nothing Austin 7 used. Forerunner of the famous Lotus 7, this car was offered in do-it-yourself (DIY) self-assembly form and established Lotus as a low-volume sports car manufacturer. 1953-55, 110 plus built.

Mark 7 A logical development of the Mark 6, the 7 is still in production today. 1957-73, then Caterham Seven, 1986.

Mark 8 Significant because it was the first Lotus that took aerodynamics into account, with its fully enveloping two-seater bodywork. A very successful sports racer. 1954-55, ten built.

Mark 9 Designed to be an improvement along the road to the Lotus Eleven, the Mark 9 was lower, lighter and more powerful, so it maintained the winning ways of the marque. 1955, twenty-three built.

Mark 10 A version of the Mark 8 modified to accommodate two-liter six-cylinder Bristol engine (BMW-based) or Connaught. 1955-56, six or seven built.

Mark 11 This stunningly beautiful two-seater ultra-aerodynamic sports car was a developed Mark 9 in two versions: Le Mans and Clubman. 1956, over 300 built (?).

Type 12 A new venture for Lotus: an open-wheeled single-seater for 1500 cc Formula 2 races. 1956-57, twelve built.

Type 13 Not used.

Type 14 The Elite. The first Lotus to have a name, and the first aerodynamic road-going coupe to pioneer glassfiber monocoque construction. 1957-63, between 990 and 1,050 built.

Type 15 A development based on the Eleven with a Lotus-designed "positive-stop" gearbox. 1958, twenty-seven built.

Type 16 This reflected state-of-the-art aerodynamics and was named the mini-Vanwall. Chapman had done consultancy work for the Vanwall and Grand Prix cars driven by Stirling Moss, and this new Lotus "shared" the research. A Formula 1/2 car, it is much in demand today for historic single-seater racing, which it dominates. 1958-59, eight cars built. There must be ten of them around today!

Type 17 A long, narrow Eleven that was not a success until a radical rework of the suspension. 1958-59, twenty-three built.

Type 18 First mid-engined Lotus single-seater destined for both Formula Junior and Formula 1! Made famous by Stirling Moss, this car had the aerodynamics of a brick and led to the 20. 1960, over 150 built, 1961 (?).

Type 19 Chapman took a hacksaw to the chassis of the 18 and widened it into a two-seater sports racer to take a two-liter (2.5/2.7 later) Climax engine. 1960-62, sixteen built. Two (19B) with American V-8s for Dan Gurney.

Type 20 As mentioned, this was a wind-cheating Lotus 18 and it reappeared years later as the Lotus 51 Formula Ford. 1961, 120 built.

Type 21 An update on the Lotus 20 Formula 1 chassis, the car was a stopgap while the new generation of Grand Prix V-8s came along from Coventry Climax. 1961, eleven built.

Type 22 Built for Formula Junior in the UK, using a Ford engine, it was also sold with the Lotus Twincam for other markets and formulas. 1962, seventy-seven built.

Type 23 Another milestone for Lotus, the 23 and 23B Twincam two-seater sports racers took the world's racetracks by storm and are still winning today. 1962-66, over 130 built then and more later!

Type 24 The last spaceframe Lotus sold to several teams who did not know that before mid-season the Lotus 25 monocoque could render them all as "also rans." 1962, at least twelve built.

Type 25 First monocoque Grand Prix car. Voted by many "the most beautiful Lotus ever," this car set new standards in Grand Prix technology and dominated Formula 1 with Jim Clark as driver. 1962, seven built.

Type 26 Enter the backbone chassis Elan. A replacement for the Elite, this car had a steel-backbone chassis, but the idea was not a result of turning a monocoque upside-down, as often suggested. 1962-73, over 12,000 built.

Type 26R Racing Elan. 1963-65, 125 built.

Type 27 The flexi-Lotus Formula Junior. This car was a disaster as its monocoque flexed so much that it was declared "undriveable." A move from fiberglass panels to aluminum solved the problem. 1963, no figures available.

Type 28 The Cortina Lotus. Cooperation between Lotus and Ford dominated sedan races and rallies worldwide. A great success and a collector car today. 1962-66, over 3,000 road-going cars built, ninety-seven pure racers.

Type 29 Another example of Lotus and Ford cooperation. This car finished second in the Indy 500 driven by Jim Clark. Based on the Lotus 25 monocoque. 1963, three built.

Type 30 A brave attempt at a V-8-powered two-seater sports car that failed. 1964, thirty-three built.

Type 31 Destined to attack the new Formula 3 one-liter class, this was a revamp of the tubular chassis Lotus 22 but other makers had produced new, faster designs! 1964, twelve built.

Type 32 Sharing the styling of its big sister, the Lotus 25, this Formula 2 car had the new one-liter Ford Cosworth SCA "screamer" engine which also appeared in Tasman series with a 2.5 liter Climax. 1964, twelve built.

Type 33 An improved version of the Lotus 25 developed with the tire manufacturers' wider treads that started the trend toward today's massive tread areas. 1964-65, seven built.

Type 34 The 1964 Indianapolis team cars that experienced suspension damage due to tire failure. 1964, three built.

Type 35 Designed as a multimarket single-seater for F2, F3 and American FB, the car was a moderate success in sales and in races. Based on the 27 and 32. 1965, twenty-two built.

Type 36 The up-market Elan Fixed Head Coupe which took Lotus into a more lucrative market and greater profitability. 1965.

Type 37 Actually known as the Lotus 3-7, it was a one-off racing Seven used by Lotus to win the British Clubman Championships after a car called the Terrier, designed by Lotus F1 man Len Terry, had won the Colin Chapman Clubman Trophy! 1965, one built.

Type 38 The Len Terry-designed 1965 Indianapolis car that won the race. It featured a "cigar tube" monocoque, as opposed to the previous "bath tub" designs. 1965, six built.

Type 39 A modified Type 33 for the Australian Tasman series in 1966, one only.

Type 40 Now famous as the "Lotus 30 with ten more mistakes" (Dan Gurney quote). 1965, three built.

Type 41 An all-out attack on the Formula 3 market saw this car win a lot of races and a lot of sales. Conventional tubular chassis marked Chapman's realization that monocoques had no place in small single-seater racing and were too expensive to make and repair. 1966, sixty-one built.

Type 42 The Indy "disaster" cars. Two were supposed to have big H16 BRM engines which never appeared after "mice had eaten the plans and thieves had stolen vital components at the last minute." 1966, two built.

Type 43 An interim F1 car using the Grand Prix version of the self-destructing BRM H16 engine. Only Lotus won a race with this engine! Chassis thought to be based on the 42 Indy car. 1966-67, two built.

Type 44 An amalgamation of Lotus 35 tub and Lotus 41 wide suspension for Formula 2 races. 1966, three built.

Type 45 The Elan Fixed Head Coupe with the top chopped off! In fact, the bodies were made in the fixed head mold, but the laminators just stopped short to leave the top off.

Type 46 The new mid-engined Renault-powered "GT-40 for the working classes," called the Europa. Backbone chassis. 1967, over 9,000 built.

Type 47 Look-alike racing car using race-tuned Lotus Twincam in a modified chassis for sports car racing—very successful if you could stop it! 1967, fifty-five built.

Type 48 The car that Clark died in. These attractive monocoque F2 cars were in no way competitive, despite John Player sponsorship at a time when all the Grand Prix drivers also drove in the F2 series on alternate weekends. 1967, four built.

Type 49 Another significant car, it was the first to use the new Cosworth DFV Grand Prix V-8, winning the first time out. Chapman eliminated all subframes to the rear of the driver by mounting everything on the engine! 1967, approximately twelve built.

Type 50 There was no celebration at the half-century, but the Elan Plus 2 opened up new markets. Alongside the Elan and the Europa, it put Lotus into substantial profits leading to a public share offer that made Chapman a millionaire. 1967, reputedly over 5,000 built.

Type 51 Derived from the Lotus 20 and 22, this bargain-basement single-seater was sold to those aspiring to greatness via the then-new Formula Ford class of racing. 1967, over 150 built.

Type 52 Prototype Twincam Europa. Never released. 1968, one built.

Type 53 Not produced. Was to be a split 51 for two-seater Sports 2000 races.

Type 54 Europa facelift (S2) with electric windows but still Renault powered. 1969-71.

Type 55 Prototype F3 car raced with JPS sponsorship. Not sold. 1968, one built.

Type 56 The four-wheel-drive Indy Turbine wedge car that made every designer and rule maker think again. Dominated the race but both cars broke a simple quill shaft to their fuel pumps in the closing stages. 1968, four built.

Type 57 This was a probe into the future using suspension of the past! A Formula 2 design exercise using DeDion suspension and a beam front axle! Abandoned. 1968, one built.

Type 58 A converted Type-57. Never raced. 1968, one built.

Type 59 Shark-nosed, multimarket single-seater for F3, F2 and US FB. Still a much-sought-after car for a historic single-seater. 1969, thirty plus built.

Type 60 The Lotus Seven Series Four, but always called by the latter name. Not a great success in its time, as it wandered too far from the Seven theme. 1969, 430 built.

Type 61 A Lotus 51 upgraded and fitted with the then-fashionable wedge-shaped bodywork. 1969, over 250 built.

Type 62 The ultimate in the Europa theme for racing, sponsored by John Player. Used Lotus' own sixteen-valve dohc two-liter but with a GM iron block. Very fast, but all manner of fins and spoilers couldn't keep it stable at high speed. 1969, two built.

Type 63 The four-wheel-drive F1 Cosworth-powered car that did not work. 1969, two built.

Type 64 Four-wheel-drive Indianapolis "wedge" with turbocharged Ford quad-cam V-8. Suspension failure sidelined the cars before the race. 1969, four built.

Type 65 Federal Renault Europa for United States. 1970.

Type 66 Not used, project unknown.

Type 67 Aborted project for Tasman series. 1970.

Type 68 Prototype of what became the Lotus 70 Formula 5000 car. Wedge shaped, of course. 1969, one built.

Type 69 Update on the 59 for F2 and F3 racing. 1970, fifty-seven built.

Type 70 Definitive F5000 but a failure. 1970, seven built.

Type 71 Not used, project unknown.

Type 72 The famous wedge-shaped F1 car with torsion bar suspension. This set new standards for Grand Prix design and maintained the cyclical Lotus dominance of F1 which had been experienced with the 25/33 and then the 49. 1970, probably nine cars built.

Type 73 Formula 3 car that was adapted to take the Lotus two-liter engine for F2 when a bundle of Texaco oil money was put up as sponsorship; a failure! 1973, two built.

Type 74 The actual cars raced for Texaco Star; also the number given to the Europa Twincam. 1970-73.

Type 75 The new Elite two-liter four-seater car that took Lotus up-market in a big way in 1974. 1974, over 3,000 built.

Type 76 Dual numbering saw this designated a disastrous replacement for the aged Lotus 72, and the Lotus Eclat 2 plus 2 known as the Sprint in the United States. 1975, over 2,500 built.

Type 77 A probe car built for one F1 season with every possible adjustability built in. One victory but it produced a lot of data. 1971, three built.

Type 78 The car that put Lotus back among the laurel leaves with Andretti. Except for mechanical faults, this car would have been as dominant as the 79. It pioneered ground effects. 1977, four built.

Type 79 The car that ran away to a succession of 1-2 victories plus the World Championship for Andretti and Constructors Championship for Lotus in 1978. (Also Esprit S1, 1975.) 1978, eight cars thought to have been built.

Type 80 A Formula 1 disaster following the success of the 79. The car was too sophisticated, too heavy and overstretched itself aerodynamically. 1979, two cars built.

Type 81 This was the Sunbeam Lotus cooperative car using the Lotus sixteen-valve dohc engine stretched to 2.2 liters in a small Chrysler Sunbeam sedan bodyshell. Also a new F1 car for Essex sponsorship in F1 but little success. 1980-81, approximately 2,000 built.

Type 82 The Esprit Turbo. 1980, over 1,000 built.

Type 83 The 2.2 version of the Elite four-seater. 1980.

Type 84 The 2.2 version of the Eclat (Sprint). 1982, 223 built.

Type 85 The 2.2 version of the Esprit S2 model. 1982, over 750 built to date.

Type 86 The controversial twin-chassis F1 car that was banned before it had even proved itself a threat to established designs! 1979-80, one built.

Type 87 A stopgap F1 car used while the lawyers argued about the Type 86. 1980, three built.

Type 88 The final, lighter, twin-chassis F1 car that still couldn't get past the rule makers. Two built.

Type 89 Not known as yet. Thought to be 4x4 (Sunbeam) Talbot Horizon. See Type 81. Also Lotus Eclat Excel in 1982.

Type 90 Prototype of the possible X100 Lotus Toyota sports car.

Type 91 First Grand Prix Lotus using composite Kevlar in the monocoque. 1982, estimated six built.

Type 92 Prototype fitted with experimental Lotus "Active Suspension System." This technology is not now being seen as a Grand Prix possibility by Lotus. 1982, two built.

Type 93 Renault Turbo-powered Grand Prix car adapted "by committee" after Chapman's death. 1983, three built.

Type 94 Reverting to the 91 as a base car, newcomer Gerard Decarouge brought out this front-runner in just a few hectic weeks. 1983, four built.

Type 95 The 1984-season car that looked good from the day of its announcement and put Lotus back among the front-runners and in the money once again. Chapman would have been pleased. Six built.

Type 96 1985 Indianapolis project.

Type 97 1985 F1 car.

Production numbers

In the years to come, researchers into the many Lotus mysteries will undoubtedly concern themselves with exactly how many of each model was made. My advice is quite simple: "Give up now!" The figures shown above are the best available, even better than those taken by various Inland Revenue inspectors over the years.

Anyone who makes tea "English style" knows that you put a spoonful of tea for every person present plus "one for the pot." This phrase was put to use at Lotus in the early days—building an extra car that either never appeared on the records or duplicated one that did. For example, researchers will come up with figures for Elan production that are greater than the actuals. There are two reasons: First, the factory claimed the higher figure for a PR puff some years ago. Examination of the records clearly shows that somebody skipped "several thousand" numbers. Second, if we take total Lotus Twincam production and deduct Lotus Cortinas, Lotus must have sold shiploads of cars without engines. But it didn't. And what the hell anyway—Lotus made the cars, not statistical records.

Those who concern themselves with the registration of a particularly rare Lotus model that reputedly never made the company a profit are becoming intrigued by the number of duplicated chassis numbers now emerging. They always report the same scenario: One is owned in Britain and the other has spent all its time in the United States. For obvious legal reasons I can't be more specific and perhaps there is a good, simple explanation as to how exactly fifty cars went to the United States when the records suggest they were sold in Britain as well!

As Lotus sales director in the mid-sixties I had to locate every unsold Lotus in the United States and attach to them new chassis plates. (It was something to do with model years and safety.) I brought hundreds of old chassis plates back to the factory, leaving the same number of Lotus cars in the United States with a whole new identity. So if you write to the Lotus factory with a chassis/unit number off one of these cars you might be told that no such number exists or was ever issued. That is because without any guidance from the factory I made up my own series of numbers while in the United States, but nobody kept a record.

One question everybody is asking is "How many Lotus cars are still running and restorable?" I came up with the following estimate after exhaustive inquiries, including some semilegal access to the British Vehicle Licensing Computer some years ago. It provided both actually licensed Lotus cars and "recent delinquents."

Mk Six	30
Mk Seven/Caterham	3,500
Eleven	50-75
Elite Climax	250
Type 23	40
Elan	3,000-4,000
Elan Plus 2	2,000-3,000
Elan Racing	40
Cortina Lotus	600-1,000
Europa	2,000-3,000

How to buy a Lotus

Some years ago a time-worn Lotus was junked without so much as a thought or regret; the classic car movement has changed all that. Today's basket-case Lotus could be tomorrow's small fortune for an enthusiastic restorer. If an owner experiences cash-flow deficiency when his Lotus needs repair, the car gets tucked away in the garage to await a change in fortune. Lotus parts suppliers report a drop in sales of brake pads, clutches, exhaust systems and other consumable parts that wear out from continual use. Demand patterns have shifted toward new chassis, frames, major engine parts, trim and so on, as the Lotus restoration movement gathers momentum.

Where racing rules permit, cars like the Lotus Elan still take on, and beat, today's cars—on equal terms. When they compete in the appropriate classes for classic and post-historic sports cars, they are also unbeatable. Older Lotus racing cars like the 23 and 23B have suddenly become like precious jewels on both sides of the Atlantic. They are *the* cars to own and run in competition.

Authentication

The first step in examining your prospective purchase is authenticating the car. This is not always easy; I know of some cases where, at the end of a very intensive search, an owner has come to the conclusion that if he can't authenticate the car, nobody else can. Therefore, it's a Lotus unless proved differently.

Obviously, the first thing to do is get the unit number from the chassis plate. It can be found in the engine bay or in the nose of the mid-engined Lotus, and will read as one of the following:

1. Former team cars: "Team Lotus"
2. Early Lotus up to type 16 and Lotus Seven: "Lotus Components Limited," "Lotus Engineering Limited" or "Lotus Racing Limited"
3. Lotus road cars: "Lotus Cars Limited"
4. Coop cars: The Cortina Lotus and Sunbeam Lotus bear the parent manufacturer's chassis-numbering scheme, Ford or Talbot respectively.

Lotus often stamped or tagged the chassis number (or unit number, as the factory called it) elsewhere on the chassis. There was no logic to the placement, so start hunting down there in the grease and rust. Also, most cars come with some documentation that can verify the car. British road cars have either a log book or a later registration certificate that lists chassis number, engine number, make and owner.

Beware of cars missing the unit number. It is easy to "fake" a Lotus under restoration with various used and new parts. In some circumstances you can get a replacement chassis plate from the factory or Club Lotus; you will have to authenticate the car to the complete satisfaction of one or the other. On the Elan, Europa, Plus 2 and later models, the unit number also appears on the inside of the door panel or sometimes on a Dymo tag set into the fiberglass in the engine bay, usually under the wiring harness. On the Elan, the number also appears under the rear bumper and inside the doors.

Once you have the actual number, you can get more information about the car from the factory. To ensure response, keep your request succinct and enclose an international mail prepayment voucher. The company can tell you when the car was made, its approximate specifications and original color, plus the name of the dealer or importer. Do not be surprised to find that for the Cortina Lotus, Elan, Europa, and Plus 2 (even Formula Ford), the original consignee was in Holland or the Bahamas. This was because Lotus and certain other individuals began shipping "grey" cars into the United States when the cars were "slightly illegal" or when US dealers had full inventories and Lotus had a low bank balance.

Club Lotus of England will assist with verification of cars. The service is free to members ($25 for nonmembers). After verifying the car, the club issues a Certificate of Verification. This is essential for entering certain classes of historic racing where you are required to prove authenticity and date of manufacture. Most major clubs may also be of help when it comes to obtaining clearance to import a Lotus that was manufactured prior to 1967 without having to meet federal or state emission and safety standards.

Inspection

If you are seriously considering the purchase of a used Lotus of any type, I recommend you check it over carefully before you agree to buy or pay a deposit fee. The following preliminaries should be considered.

1. Exact description of the car as claimed by the seller.
   Year: Model: Engine:
2. Does the seller have the title to the car?
3. Does the seller have authority to sell the car *today*?
4. What documentation exists to verify the car?
5. What chassis plates or other identification can be found?
6. Does information in (5) check with (4)?
7. Does the description in (1) check with what you see?

There are also many specific areas to check while the car is sitting still. Remember that it's important to do a thorough job here and, above all, take your time!

Walk around the car from at least fifteen feet away and look at it from each quarter position to determine if it is sitting level and looks "straight." Then slowly go over all of the bodywork looking for damage, poor repairs and the like. Next, check the condition of all glass, sidecurtains and roll-up windows including the plexiglass in a soft top.

Verify that all five wheels match, are in good shape and are fitted with the proper tires. And, be sure that all bumpers, lights, trim strips and badges are correct and in place.

Check the condition of the interior carefully, noting the instruments, switches and trim. You'll also need to inspect inside the trunk for soft top, tools, spare wheel and the condition of the gas tank (any gasoline smell or pools of gas?). Another area to check is under the hood for obvious signs of oil leaks, faulty wiring, coolant loss; note if the engine is hot or cold. Sniff for smell of hot oil or hot antifreeze, burnt electrics and gasoline. Note condition of oil and check all fluids.

Test all lights, switches, instruments, radio, wipers, turn indicators, heater, hand brake and foot brake. On Lotus cars with pop-up headlights check to see they work, and drive with them up to check durability of the system.

Get under the car with as much light as possible! Go slowly down the car looking for chassis rust, fluid leaks, damage, signs of poor maintenance or a recent cover-up job. Don't be afraid to probe with a sharp tool and pull on all joints. Examine the inside wall of each tire; inspect springs and shocks; check the gas tank; trace hydraulic and fuel lines and exhaust system and handbrake cables. Inspect obvious underpan wiring.

You will also want to check the inside of body panels for extra fiberglass laminate. This is a sure sign that a body repair has taken place. The most likely areas to receive damage are the front, the rear and in the quarters. Inspecting these areas will tell you just how much has been repaired, especially on Europa, Elan, Elan Plus 2, Esprit Elite and Eclat (Sprint). If you find a large, new section of fiberglass, it should be attached to an LR-series Lotus replacement chassis. The use of fiberglass means that distortion and damage was local to the impact. A professionally repaired Lotus can be as good as the day it was built. New bodywork can be molded in and be even stronger than the original.

On some early Lotus models, you may have to find out if the car has the more desirable ZF gearbox or a standard Austin, Ford or MG unit. The more sophisticated ZFs had an alloy casing, so don't be fooled by an MG gearbox with a ZF shift knob. Look for obvious oil leaks and determine their origin. Some oil leaks can be quick and inexpensive to repair, others can spell financial ruin. For example, a new block or expensive aluminum build-up may be required on the Coventry Climax engine.

Road test

Your road test, if the car is running, should be lengthy and thorough. Note oil pressure and water temperature when just starting the engine. Start off slowly and immediately check brakes and steering. Listen for clutch noise or any changes in noises as you pull away, such as clicks, jerks or rattles.

Take the car up through the gears, using moderate revs, until the whole unit is well warmed-up. Take a reading of oil pressure, temperature, generator charge and so on. Do the speedometer and tachometer read accurately and steady? After checking the mirror, brake rather hard to a stop. Does the car stop in a straight line? Now take off briskly, using ninety percent of the permitted revs in all gears. Does the car pull to one side during acceleration and duck to the other during gear shifts?

After stopping again, accelerate away. Before up-shifting, take your foot off the gas so all overrun forces go through the gearbox. Does the car pop out of gear? Do this in all four (or five) forward speeds.

Note all vibrations, rattles and strange noises. Think positively and plan to investigate them later. Then, take the car fast and hard into a corner and lift your foot off the gas in the apex. Does the car lurch, dive or go off line? Accelerate hard out of a turn and feel for any changes of attitude, rear end breakaway or excess sway.

Be sure to recheck oil pressure and water temperature readings. Assuming you have access to a track or feel a bit gutsy on an open road, hold the car at around 100 mph for at least two miles. Keep an eye on the oil pressure and water temperature and listen for mechanical noises from bearing knock or gear whine.

At the end of your road test, drive the car for several miles as you would normally drive it. When you stop, check for oil or water leaks at the engine. Ask yourself if this is the car you thought it was from magazines (and this book). Do you like it and do you want to purchase it, considering the asking price?

Making the decision

Ask the seller for service records; careful owners keep copies of invoices and service history. After five years a Lotus car is more a product of its previous owner than the factory. Well serviced and using genuine parts and factory-trained mechanics make a true Lotus. Repaired by a gorilla and raced on weekends by a poverty-stricken student, the car will become a "dog" in a short time. A Lotus is a finely tuned machine that requires costly upkeep. The absence of records tells you somebody didn't have the caring concern for the car. These records will also be helpful if you later sell the car.

If you are looking at a basket case, do not underestimate how much of the car is missing. If the car is partially restored, I would advise you to choose a car in good mechanical condition, as opposed to choosing one for its paint job and trim. Many people (and salesmen) know the seductive influence of a paint job, so don't get taken!

If all is well, start talking dollars with the seller. However, if you are looking for later Lotus cars and have a choice of more than one car, do not fall in love with the first one you see. Take your time, unless you find exactly what you want at a price that fits your budget.

Chapter 1

Six and Seven

The Lotus Six and Seven are essentially the same animal from a design point of view; one is just the forerunner of the other. Both were major winners on the racetrack.

The Lotus Six plays a significant role in the history of Lotus—it was the company's first production car. The Sixes were all roughly the same thereafter because Chapman "froze" the design to enable the Progress Chassis Company of Edmonton in North London to build jigs and then work with their neighbors, Williams & Pritchard, the aluminum body panel specialists, who "productionized" the bodies.

The Six and Seven feature carefully calculated, triangulated spaceframe chassis giving light weight and enormous torsional rigidity. The cars are very stark and simple,

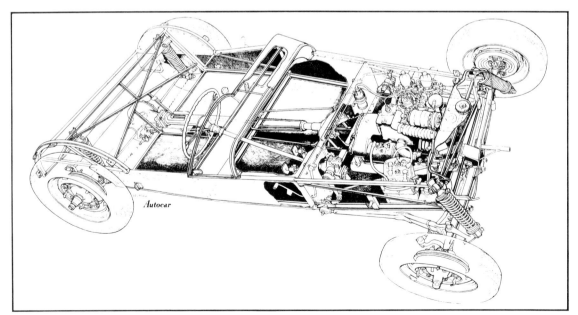

Lotus Six cutaway. The car was stark and simple in the extreme. The Lotus Six and the Mercedes-Benz 300SLR were the only truly stressed space-framed cars in those days! Note split front axle. Business Press International Ltd.

	Fun	*Investment*	*Anguish*
Lotus Six	8	10	3
Lotus Seven	8	10	3

having been designed to meet the then-English-club racing tradition that called for the car to be driven to the circuit under its own power. In fact, the regulations of the original 750 formula, where Chapman ruled supreme with the Mk 3 forerunner to the Six, actually stated the car had to be "capable" of this. Many cars were scrutinized if they arrived on trailers.

The Six was designed with an engine bay that would accept almost any small, light-weight high-performance engine, from a humble side-valve Ford 1172 to a Conventry Climax. The pushrod Ford Consul four-

Ford "side-valve" 1172 engine in a Six. It was the backbone of English club racing in the 1950s. Chapman used it often in his Six and Seven. *Road & Track*

MODEL	Lotus Six		Panhard rod. Drum brakes all round. Burman box-type steering.
YEARS PRODUCED	1952/53-1955/56		
BODY & CONFIGURATION	Front engine, rear drive, 2-seater open sports. Very basic. Alloy panels. Integral body chassis.	**ENGINE**	Anything from Ford side-valve 1172 cc, Austin A-series. MG TD 1497 cc ohc. Coventry Climax ohc 1100 cc.
PURPOSE	Fun road car and club races.		
CHASSIS & SUSPENSION	Tubular-steel triangulated spaceframe reinforced via stressed floor panel, propshaft tunnel and firewall. Independent front suspension via split Ford beam and combined coil springs and shock absorbers. Rear via Ford hypoid-bevel solid axle on combined coil springs and telescopic shock absorbers with	**TRANSMISSION**	Ford, Austin or MG 3- or 4-speed. 15-inch wire or pressed-steel wheels.
		NOTES	This was a true Lotus kit car and most customers bought their engines from other sources. Lotus did not mind what the customer fitted but frowned on big American V-8s. The same applied to gearboxes.

cylinder, the MG ohc and the various Austin (BMC) A-series engines were also popular. Being a kit car in every sense of the word, a lot of customers either already owned a suitable engine or had a cheaper source than Lotus. There is, therefore, no "purist's" list of approved engine installations and I have seen Sixes fitted with contemporary Fiat, Alfa Romeo and many other units.

Chapman took an early dislike to the car, as it was not as profitable as he would have liked; especially as the complicated bodywork was carried out by Williams & Pritchard who also wanted to make a small profit. The chassis may have been a mathematical triumph but it was also expensive to produce. All these financial constraints led Chapman to design the Seven, which would have a simple chassis and simple, low-cost panels with no more than the occasional double curvature. It has been noted by many commentators on the history of racing car

A Lotus Six wins again, 1984. Driver was Chris Smith (Westfield Cars). Club Lotus England

The attractive backside of the original Lotus Six. Chapman said the panels cost too much! This is Chris Smith's car in 1979. Club Lotus England

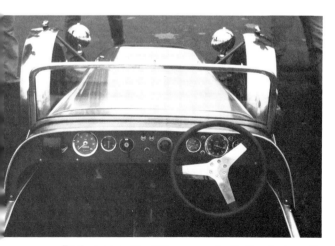

Early Lotus Six Climax cockpit. Car is heavily restored. Club Lotus England

Early Lotus Six rear axle layout. Club Lotus England

design that Chapman's Lotus Six had a chassis that was only equaled in brilliance and calculated stresses by no less an opus than the 300SLR that took Mercedes-Benz back to the pinnacle of sports car racing in the 1950s. (Chapman would never have put a swing axle rear suspension in any of his creations!) Finally, the Tipo 61 Birdcage Maserati made nonsense of the whole idea just as the monocoque concept appeared.

A nice, clean Lotus Six ready to race at Laguna Seca in 1986. Guess the rollbar doesn't do much for looks. Tim Parker

Silverstone and the 6-Hours Relay in 1953 with the "works" team of Lotus Sixes. Note the expensive, handcrafted rear fenders. Chapman "dropped" them on the Seven for cheaper, "flat" panels.

Engine bay of a very rare Climax-engined Lotus Six. It just fits. Graham Hill raced a DeDion back-end version to many victories. Club Lotus England

A Lotus Six that is for sale is now such a rarity that any reader locating one should contact Club Lotus or the Historic Lotus Register for verification and guidance—in total confidence, of course. If asked what to look for, I would say, "a chassis plate that says it is a Lotus Six; after that only the price is of any importance."

The Seven was designed to house a new generation of engines, mostly Ford based, plus the Climax unit fitted to the Elite. Eventually, it appeared with the Lotus Big Valve Sprint Twincam.

Despite what purists would like to think, Colin Chapman did not care a bit for the Lotus Seven. Instant dismissal was the threatened fate for anyone who made suggestions for updates or improvements. Developments were only made if a supplier refused to deliver due to nonpayment, or if a

Ford 1600 crossflow with twin Weber 40DC0E7s. Lotus Seven Series 1. Club Lotus England

Lotus Seven Series 2 as featured in the famous television series *The Prisoner*. Patric McGoohan (left) and Graham Nearn, of Caterham Cars. Club Lotus England

major component went out of production. Lotus went from a Triumph rear axle to Ford only when the supply dried up.

The Caterham connection

The exclusive distributor for Great Britain was and is Caterham Cars Limited, near London (which also manufactured derivatives of the car, including a Ford Cosworth sixteen-valve Twincam version equipped with DeDion rear end and other improvements.) Only Caterham's repeat orders kept the car alive, especially after the Series Four proved to be a lemon in terms of sales. Now it is in great demand.

In 1971, Lotus Components Limited, renamed Lotus Racing, was shut down by a stroke of Chapman's pen, and Graham Nearn of Caterham Cars saw his chance. He approached Lotus for an agreement to manufacture the car under license. Many claim that all this agreement consisted of was a shake of the hand. However, there was one other known provision: Nearn had to buy 100 surplus Lotus 61M Formula Ford racing cars. It is also suggested that the agreement was actually only to produce the Seven Series Four and provide "product support" for the Series Three cars, the Super Sevens.

Whatever the legalities and requirements, this was all finally sorted out by 1984 with a proper license from Lotus making the Caterham Seven the only officially recognized

Class winner at Brighton Speed Trials, on the English south coast. This car was registered in 1964 and has neat Minilite wheels.

Lotus Seven—what every young person wants—but only their fathers can afford.

American Seven racer at Laguna Seca during the vintage races in 1986. Are they Minilites or the later Panasport wheels? Tim Parker

First production Seven Series 4 at Hethel. Chapman later denied all knowledge of it.

Seven Series 4 cockpit. Note comprehensive dials and molded dash.

Lotus Seven in the world today. There are, however, many replicas and look-alikes in the Seven market.

Nearn started to build the Caterham Seven in 1973 and now his production lines supply these exciting cars to the entire world. His updated versions, "logically developed from the spirit of the Seven," are based on the Series Three Super Seven, although he still provided full product support for the Series Four. The following chart sums up the production history of the Seven.

Lotus Seven
Series 1
Production   1957-60
Number built   Approximately 250
Chassis numbers   400-499 (built at Hornsey)
                     750-892 (built at Cheshunt)

Note the differences. A Lotus Seven Series 2 (left) alongside a Series 4 (right). The Seven Series 2 appears to have something massive under the hood. Club Lotus England

Series 2
Production   October 1960-June 1968
Number built   1,370

Series 3
Production   1968-70
Number built   Approximately 350
Chassis numbers   2101 onward
   Note: Suffix SB and SC for Twincam, Suffix L for left-hand-drive export car

Series 4
Production   1970-73
Number built   Approximately 1,000
   Note: Suffix SB and SC for Twincam, Suffix L for left-hand-drive export car

Caterham 7
Production   1974 onward
Number built   Estimated over 5,000
Chassis numbers   CS3/ . . . onward (built at Caterham)
   Note: All built under license

Lotus Seven Series 4 Twincam engine bay. This engine fits easily, even as a retrofit in the S3 or S4.

Lotus Seven Series 4 Twincam. Nonstandard and much later wheels. Club Lotus England

What to look for

When considering either a Lotus Six or Seven (as I've already stated, if it's a Six, buy it anyway), there really isn't all that much to care a lot about. Check for chassis straightness, rust and bad repairs (especially welding), rippled bodywork and missing badges. Because the Caterham Seven is still being made, there is essentially a source of supply that isn't about to run out. Mechanical checks are the standard ones you would apply to any car.

Driving impressions

Lotus Seven spells excitement—the excitement of noise, wind rushing past your face, and raw acceleration with spinning wheels and white tire smoke—all from around 100 bhp. The Seven is a car with no real creature comforts, an apology for a heater, water leaks everywhere and luggage space enough for a bikini and two toothbrushes.

The Lotus Seven is a race car on the road. It rockets away from stoplights, turns corners like a single-seater formula car and stops quickly and predictably, even in the wet. (Weather is not its enemy as long as it stays dry and in the high 70s.) The gearbox is such a delight that you'll downshift just to hear the beautiful sound of that tearing exhaust and the thirsty gulpings of those twin-choke Weber carburetors. The ride is rock firm, unlike any other Lotus built to the Chapman tradition of a soft ride with progressive damping. The Seven and its ancestors have been around for thirty years and will continue forever if some people in England have their way.

The "kit car" explained

The origins of the "kit car" in Britain are simple. In the postwar years, the main sales tax was levied on some products but not others. Luxury items were highly taxed and certain essentials bore no tax at all. A car was considered a luxury and had the burden of a very high tax level, sometimes as much as

The Caterham Seven has a stronger, stiffer chassis, especially around the front suspension. This is a 1985 chassis. Caterham Cars Ltd

Ford engine, possibly a former Formula Ford unit, in a Lotus Seven Caterham.

thirty-three percent. However, car parts, essential to people's mobility, were not taxed.

Chapman and other sports car and specialty builders had two problems. The first was that the last five percent of the required assembly work took up to fifty percent of the time and was therefore expensive. Second, low-volume cars built on a one-by-one basis were obviously more expensive in terms of parts and labor costs than a production-line MG or Morgan, for instance.

So Chapman decided to sell his Lotus Six partially assembled, arguing that since they were sports racing cars the owner should follow a time-honored tradition and get to know the car by building it. During this time, Stirling Moss spent several weeks at the Maserati factory with his mechanic, Alf Francis, doing just that. Since the cars were sold in pieces, they avoided tax and they therefore cost less.

Chapman asked the local tax officer how many supply sources had to be used to build a car out of spare parts. "More than one and no less than two," came the bureaucratic reply. So Chapman sold the car in two bundles, the chassis body unit came from Lotus Engineering Ltd. and the remainder from Racing Engines Limited. Once you had made your purchase you would unpack all the pieces to find a long list of items marked "Out of stock, to follow soon."

This kit car "loophole" in Britain's tax laws turned out to be the basis of Chapman's fortunes. Even today, British government officials look kindly on what has now become a growth industry, with several new firms expanding alongside traditional com-

State of the art. The current-model Caterham Seven.

The line continues with a slightly different version of a 1986 Caterham Seven. Note the cycle wings for this European left-hand-drive version.

MODEL	Lotus Seven	**ENGINE**	Everything from 1172 side-valve Ford through Ford 998 ohv, 1340 ohv and 1500 ohv; Coventry Climax 1100 cc; BMC/Austin A-series 997 cc; and eventually Lotus Twincam in Series IV.
YEARS PRODUCED	1957-		
BODY & CONFIGURATION	Front engine, rear drive, 2-seater open sports. Very basic. Alloy and fiberglass panels. "Cycle type" fenders on earlier models gave way to US-preferred "clam shell" design. Integral body chassis.		
PURPOSE	Fast road use with some competition in mind.	**TRANSMISSION**	Ford 3-speed, then a variety of Ford 4-speed all-synchromesh, including Lotus-Ford close-ratio. Hypoid-bevel final drive using Triumph, then Ford, then Morris solid rear axle with combined coil springs and shock absorbers with radius rods. Drum brakes all round, then front discs. 15-inch pressed-steel or wire wheels on very early models, then 13-inch pressed-steel.
CHASSIS & SUSPENSION	Tubular-steel square and round section triangulated chassis with extra rigidity from stressed undertray, propshaft tunnel and engine firewall. Independent front suspension with upper and lower links and combined coil spring and shock absorber. Rear suspension solid axle with coil and shock absorber combined, plus twin parallel trailing arms and diagonal member.		
		NOTES	This car was also offered in kit form, without engine, and attracted a very wide range of innovative installations.

Caterham Cars workshops in south London in 1985. Full equipment on this version. Club Lotus England

panies like MG, Jaguar and Morgan. The industry has created jobs and wealth as well as prestige for Britain.

The kit car died when a flat fifteen percent Value Added Tax was introduced in the mid-70s. Then kit cars came back as a means of avoiding the onerous construction safety and antipollution laws in many countries. In Britain today there are many kit-car manufacturers who sell component parts —even the Caterham Seven comes that way if requested. Caterham has even had the car legalized and the type approved in many countries, including the very difficult German TUV.

A luxury version of the Caterham Seven by Avon Coachworks in England. Is it better? Club Lotus England

Vegantune Twincam engines ready for Caterham. Not sure they should be resting on the carburetors.

The Westfield 7 look-alike. "Q" plate means it's a kit-car registration. Back to the simplest? Eight-spoke wheels aren't Minilites.

Prepared for Pikes Peak—a really fast Lotus Seven. What about all that dust into those carburetor mouths?

The Seven makes a good hillclimb car. This is the project car run by *Thoroughbred and Classic Cars* magazine. Club Lotus England

The world's most famous Lotus Seven, The Black Brick, winning at Thruxton, in England, in the hands of Rob Cox. Behind is the Porsche Carrera of Barry Robinson and three-liter Marcos of Richard Gamble. This car is a phenomenon—close to 300 hp, formula car aerodynamics and much clever chassis work.

Chapter 2

Eleven

The Lotus Eleven, introduced in 1956, was a logical development from the very successful Mark 9 which was based on the first aerodynamic Lotus, the Mark 8. The Eleven's highly efficient lightweight spaceframe was clothed in one of the most beautiful hand-formed aluminum bodies ever designed.

The chassis was a carefully calculated selection of 1 inch and ¾ inch, 18 or 20 gauge steel tubes. Extra torsional stiffness was achieved by making the drive shaft tunnel an

Recorded date on this photograph is March 1957. A Lotus Eleven on test with *Road & Track*.

Note the street tires, the rearview mirror and the Exide battery in the rear. *Road & Track*

	Fun	*Investment*	*Anguish*
Lotus Eleven	7	10	6

MODEL	Lotus Eleven (type 61)
YEARS PRODUCED	1956-?
BODY & CONFIGURATION	2-seater, open cockpit, front engine, rear drive in aluminum. Front and rear body sections demountable. Drop-down doors, ducted radiator.
PURPOSE	Racing and fast road use.
CHASSIS & SUSPENSION	Triangulated tubular steel with stressed undertray, propshaft tunnel and firewall. Lotus swing axle front suspension, solid or DeDion rear end (rack and pinion steering).
ENGINE	1100 or 1500 cc Coventry Climax.
TRANSMISSION	Austin-based 4-speed, then MG axle ratios (5.1 to 3.9). 500x15 tires on Dunlop spoked center-lock wheels. Discs all round. Inboard on Le Mans.
NOTES	Two basic models: Solid rear end, Club and DeDion rear end, Le Mans with head fairing.

integral, stressed part of the chassis (as on the later Seven). The car was offered in three specifications in either completed or kit form: Sports, Club and Le Mans models.

The Sports model had a swing-axle independent front suspension, beam rear axle; outboard drum brakes all around; Ford 100E 1172 side-valve engine with three-speed gearbox.

The Club model used the same front suspension as the Sports model; Coventry Climax FWE engine with MGA gearbox; optional 1100 cc or 1460 cc Climax engines.

The Le Mans model again had the same front suspension as the Sports model; outboard disc brakes at front, inboard at rear; rear suspension was Chapman-designed DeDion tube with pierced section to facilitate halfshaft layout; fairing behind driver's head.

Although this innovative car was obviously designed to win races at all levels, the cockpit was actually complete and proved to be acceptable to sporting owners who just wanted to drive the cars on the road in good weather. There was even a map pocket, and the dash was covered in matching material. Side flaps hinged at the lower edge served as

Historic racing in England in 1980. Jaguar Drivers Club meeting at Silverstone: Le Mans Eleven leads an Elite.

doors, and a vulnerable wraparound plexiglass windshield was available to improve aerodynamics in serious competition.

All three models were available with fifteen-inch, spoked Dunlop center-lock splined wire wheels fitted with 4.5x15 front and 5.0x15 rears. Both front and rear sections of the bodywork were hinged and could be removed in seconds for major mechanical work.

In 1956, the company extended the line of Elevens available. Those engines could be fitted to several models, as follows:

Sports 45: Ford engine, live rear axle, drum brakes
Sports 75: Climax engine
Le Mans 85: Climax engine, disc brakes, DeDion axle, wishbone front suspension
Le Mans 150: Climax 1500 engine with twin overhead cams, specifications matching the Le Mans 85

The Lotus Eleven proved successful for many famous race car drivers, including Jimmy Clark, Graham Hill and Jim Hall. In 1957, a special Le Mans Eleven was built to attack records on the banked Monza circuit in Italy. This car, driven by Stirling Moss, featured an enclosed bubble top for the driver only. The car achieved a best lap of 143 mph (not bad for 1100 cc) and 100 miles at 137.5 mph, plus a crop of other records.

Lotus Eleven Le Mans. Well restored. W. Friend

Lotus Eleven at Goodwood, England, after restoration. W. Friend

Lotus Eleven chassis during restoration. Neat simplicity and familiar Dunlop racing tires. W. Friend

Lotus Eleven minus body. Shows off header tank, gas tank and twin-barrel Webers. W. Friend

The attempt was finally aborted when the battery mountings broke due to the rough out banking. Records show more than 150 Lotus Elevens were produced, with sixty-four going to the United States.

What to look for

When examining a potential purchase, satisfy yourself that the car is a genuine Lotus Eleven and not a copy by using the authenticity methods described earlier. Then see if it has a DeDion rear suspension or beam axle as in the Le Mans or Club. The body should be aluminum, not fiberglass. Look carefully—a very good but obvious replica is made by Westfields in England.

Check the chassis tubes closely for signs of twisting, fatigue, major repairs, nonstan-

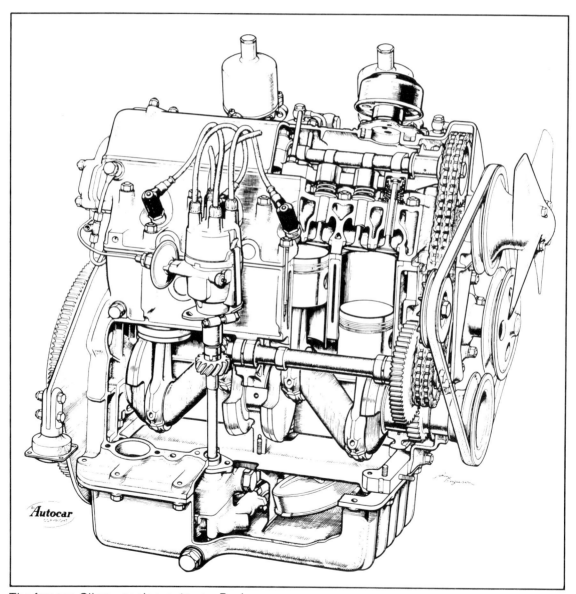

The famous Climax engine, cutaway. Business Press International Ltd

dard inserts and, above all, *rust*. Cars fitted with a Climax engine should also be checked closely, as value reflects condition. Look for cracked or shaved heads and cracked blocks. If the car has a more mundane Austin-Healey Sprite or English Ford engine, not as much scrutiny is necessary. Also, be sure to check the radiator for cracks or blockage.

In cars such as the Lotus Six and Eleven, Chapman offered two varieties. The high-specification version might have a Climax engine and a ZF gearbox, while the cheaper model would have a mundane side-valve Ford engine and a less expensive Ford or MGA/Austin gearbox. The reasons were simple. Chapman wanted a car with the specifications of a potential race winner but he also needed a car that looked identical to the other to ensure a reasonable sales volume. The lower-specification cars sold at a profitable price. It should also be remembered that the profit margin on the higher-specification exotic versions was much higher, or the discount could be greater.

Driving impressions

A contemporary writer describes his first ride in a Lotus Eleven with the Climax engine as "A Lotus Seven with a softer ride, even more air in the hair and a beautiful body." I agree.

First impressions of the cockpit are not very pleasing, however, with bare aluminum, a hint of vinyl and a small array of simple switches clustered randomly around a minimum of instruments. Fire up the motor and all hell breaks loose because the exhaust emerges from directly below the driver's door. And all Climax engines have a distinctive chatter and valve gear thrash.

Engage the rather agricultural, unsynchronized first gear of the MG gearbox, wind it up to 6000 rpm, drop the clutch and away it goes! Even on the narrow Dunlop race tires the back end digs in and it goes

Lotus Eleven Le Mans restoration almost completed. Here's how it should be done. W. Friend

An Eleven with full-width windshield, and street legal (Elan on the right). These cars are great fun.

Lotus Eleven plus spare bodyshell. Contrast the two styles—Le Mans on the right. Vic Thomas, Historic Lotus Register, UK

Climax engine with twin Webers in Lotus Eleven. Here you can see the steering rack to the right. Club Lotus England

hard and straight with the front end dipping between shifts. The clatter of the overhead cam engine combined with the sucking of the unsilenced SUs adds to the experience.

The wind pressure surrounding your head is breathtaking. Hit a curve at 110, toe the brakes, drop it into a lower gear and floor the accelerator for a fast trip over the horizon. This is an example of how the wide track and true Lotus suspension provide real opportunities for exploration to the adventurer or safety to the foolhardy.

Some say the car has no doors, and certainly Colin Chapman's duck feet, as opposed to gullwings, get some funny looks. The doors drop outward after lifting a simple catch on the wraparound plexiglass screen. More often than not, however, a clumsy passenger breaks the screen and then steps on the door. Before inviting a passenger for a ride, be sure to give him or her a quick training course in entry and exit of a Lotus Eleven.

Going racing at Laguna Seca, California, in 1986. Rivet line on the left fender suggests a repair. Tim Parker

Headlamp removal is a popular modification for Elevens. The obligatory rollbar is better shaped in this car. Tim Parker

Chapter 3

Elite (Climax)

Colin Chapman was fascinated by structures and saw the separation of chassis and bodyshell as a waste of weight. He was also keenly interested in fiberglass-reinforced resin as a potential structural material. "Why not make a fiberglass monocoque two-seater GT?" he asked. The answer to this question was the beautiful Climax-engined Elite.

I say beautiful because every car that captured Chapman's full imagination and dedication proved to be a truly elegant solution to the engineering and ergonomic problems presented to the design team. The Elite eventually did incorporate some steel subframes and windshield aperture reinforcement, but it was as near to a pure fiberglass

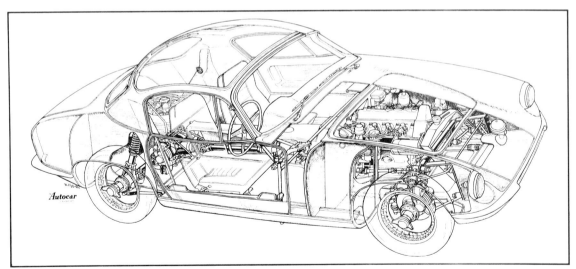

Lotus Elite cutaway drawing from Business Press International Ltd. first appeared in The Autocar. Note lack of chassis and in-board rear discs.

	Fun	Investment	Anguish
Lotus Elite (Climax)	6	10	6

monocoque as could be achieved before such exotic materials as carbon fiber and Kevlar appeared twenty-five years later. Despite the use of some metal subframes at high-load input points, Chapman varied the thickness of the laminate in other areas in direct proportion to the load-bearing needs. This meant that some areas were ¾ inch thick and others were paper thin. Such was Chapman's dedication to weight reduction that the final version of the car weighed about 1,300 pounds.

Designed by Chapman, John Frayling and Peter Kirwan-Taylor, the original prototype car shown at London's Earls Court Show in 1957 had been built from fifty-eight separate molds; however, this was reduced to three when the car went into production. The torsional rigidity achieved by this car has never been equaled by a production Lotus.

Approximately 986 Lotus Elites were built during its six years of production. A few more cars were later built when stock bodyshells were fitted with Ford or Lotus Twincams. Almost fifty additional cars were rumored to have "slipped out the rear exit," or had been built strictly from parts.

Chapman was frequently bored with a new project toward the end of its completion. As with the original Lotus Europa, no real consideration was given to windows in the Elite. This was also due to Chapman's feeling that windows should not open, thereby destroying the aerodynamics.

The Elite had rigid plexiglass windows which could be completely removed and stored in special bags behind the seats. The tumble-home of the body shape made it impossible to incorporate roll-up windows. Chapman always *hoped* that someone would develop a totally transparent, flexible material that would roll around corners!

The suspension in the Elite was identical to the "soft rider" suspension in the Lotus Twelve single-seater. This was used because Chapman was so pleased with its performance. This, possibly for the first time, was

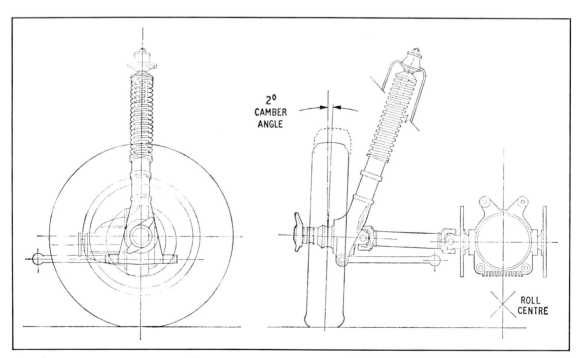

The Chapman strut was made famous on the Lotus Elite. The fixed-length drive shaft provides lateral location.

a suspension that gave the race car driver an enjoyable ride, yet enabled him to experience it from out front.

American-market Elite with left-hand drive. Very simple but complicated. *Road & Track*

Chapman's appreciation of the structure's shortcomings also called for the widest possible separation of pick-up points. The front end was controlled by a double-wishbone setup using fabricated tubular steel wishbones and a steeply raked coil spring and shock-absorber unit. A lot of rubber was used to reduce the amount of road rumble in the cockpit.

The front brakes were 9½ inch discs with alloy calipers, or cast iron on later cost-cutter models. Dunlop fifteen-inch wire wheels originally carried 4.50x15 Firestone P100 cable-stitch-pattern tires or 5.00x15 Michelin X or Pirelli Cinturato.

The Elite utilized the highly respected Alford & Adler high-ratio rack-and-pinion steering. Despite the docile ride, in later models an even softer setting for springs and dampers was adopted which increased the ultimate road holding.

The rear suspension featured the famous Chapman strut. It had a high-mounted top pick-up point and traditional long stroke through the combined spring and shock absorber. The independently sprung, universally jointed drive shafts formed an integral part of the rear triangulation, needing only a kinked trailing arm to complete the

A one-owner new Elite, back at the Lotus factory for service. Note the twin tail pipes.

Elite Climax engine bay. Special Equipment model with twin SUs. Newly restored. Club Lotus England

Lotus Elite Super 95. Two-tone paint tells much. Miles Wilkins, Fibreglass Services

system. As on the front, 9½ inch discs handled the rear braking, and rubber bushes were used to absorb some of the harsher vibrations and road noises.

Second series models adopted a revised rear-suspension locating system, with the kinked trailing arm replaced by a simple wishbone system joined to the body/chassis by a fragile, rubber-insulated ball-and-socket joint.

The Coventry Climax all-alloy, single overhead camshaft engine has become part of motoring history. Its reported origin as a unit for a fire pump, like so many of those anecdotal stories, contains a grain of truth. Those involved in its production knew full well that their engine had amazing potential for cars and even boats. However, the only crock of gold to plunder was in a defense contract for a fire pump engine.

Elite Type 14 changes

Date	Change
October 1957	Prototype makes its debut at London Motor Show
December 1958	Beginning of production deliveries
July 1960	Series 2 cars in production using Bristol-built bodies
October 1960	Special Equipment version announced
May 1962	Super 95 version announced
February 1963	Super 100 announced to dealers but not officially announced to public; only six built
September 1963	Production officially ends; last car goes to Homer Rader of Texas

At least twenty Climax-engined Elites were specifically built for racing at all levels. These works cars enjoyed great success at Le Mans and Sebring, alongside cars entered by dealers and private owners. Racing bodyshells were lighter, and some featured the Costin nose. The most famous of these cars was DAD 10 (the British registration number), Les Leston's red car, which has recently been fully restored and is racing successfully in Europe.

Most cars built for road use could be raced competitively by their owners merely by adding an oil cooler, racing brake pads and competition tires.

Genuine racing Elites can be recognized by flush-fitting windshield glass, lighter-than-standard doors and other nonstressed body panels.

Chapman often said that Lotus lost money on every Elite made. But, as during the time of production, his personal wealth was secured and Lotus purchased a large new production facility north of London.

Lotus Elite interior. This time, a UK car. Note large steering wheel and the tiny dim switch on the floor. Miles Wilkins, Fibreglass Services

An unrestored Elite, believed ex-Stirling Moss, awaits auction in Monterey, California. NACA duct tells us something. Tim Parker

MODEL	Lotus Elite (Type 14)	**ENGINE**	Coventry Climax FWE 1216 cc ohc. Single SU, then twin SUs, then twin Webers on the Super 95. A few spare bodies were fitted with Twincam engines in 1968-69.
YEARS PRODUCED	1957-1963/64		
BODY & CONFIGURATION	All fiberglass, 2-seater coupe, front engine, rear drive monocoque construction with separate luggage trunk at rear. Removable side windows. Very aerodynamic by any standards.		
		TRANSMISSION	MG 4-speed or ZF all-synchromesh close-ratio. Hypoid-bevel drive differential. 15-inch wire wheels. Disc brakes all round, inboard at rear.
PURPOSE	Fast touring, not racing.		
CHASSIS & SUSPENSION	No chassis. Rack and pinion steering. Independent front suspension by wishbone and combined coil spring, shock absorber and antisway bar. Independent rear suspension by Chapman, strut coil spring, shock absorber and trailing arm.	**NOTES**	This car set new standards of performance, road holding and aesthetic design. Chapman did not want it to be raced but was forced to develop a racing version. The rest is history.

What could possibly make this group turn their backs on an Elite Climax? Club Lotus England

What to look for

The Elite had no real chassis, so the subframe is one of the most important things to inspect. The metal subframes may be starting to show signs of serious corrosion, and they are not easy to remove or replace without major surgery. The strength of the load-bearing fiberglass has also probably started to deteriorate, especially in areas of excess resin or resin starvation in the original construction. Check the stressed areas to see that the fiberglass has not broken away; this happens quite frequently around the suspension.

The bodywork has sometimes been modified to accommodate wider tires for racing or for a "macho" appearance. Beware of poor fiberglass work and poor accident repairs. As with the Eleven, check the Climax engine for problems and look for fatigue or cracks in the hub castings. The drop-out side windows and front and rear bumpers are often missing or damaged.

Driving impressions

Some say that Colin Chapman designed and built cars before noise was invented. The Elite is no exception. Inside this beautiful coupe body every decibel and vibration is magnified many times over because noise

Climax engine in Elite Super 95. Note twin Webers. Club Lotus England

Elites at a Club Lotus meet, 1985. Car on far right has drilled-out knock-off hubcap, something commonly done to save weight.

and vibration-creating components are bolted or bonded directly to the monocoque shell. It is like being inside the sounding box of a Stradivarius violin being played by a three-year-old. However, once moving, the Elite is soon forgiven.

The car's good looks attract attention but the handling and fine balance is something to savor. An Elite feels more "up on its toes" than later sporting Lotus cars because of its fifteen-inch wheels and rather high stance. However, there is no body roll at all—not even in the fastest turns.

Brake pressure is heavy by today's standards due to the absence of a servo but there is more than enough stopping power available. It certainly gets no aerodynamic braking effect from the body design. The car can be run up to 100 mph on a flat road, then with the engine off it will maintain that speed for quite a while and only gradually slow down.

Aesthetically, the interior of the Elite, like the Eleven, is rather basic, if not spartan.

The most famous Elite of all time, DAD 10. Rediscovered and back racing after being "lost" for over 15 years. Note Costin nose and smooth windshield surround. Malcolm Ricketts

In Elite company. Club Lotus stand at classic car meet.

The shape of the dashboard, door trim and so on are just right, even by today's standards, but the interior is covered with some imitation toad skin and the rest looks like the protective gray fire coating paint used on the walls in a cheap hotel—perhaps it was.

Nice Elite setup for racing at Laguna Seca in 1986, although it still has bumpers, glass and more heavyweight equipment. Tim Parker

One solution to Climax engine shortages: Mazda rotary in an Elite.

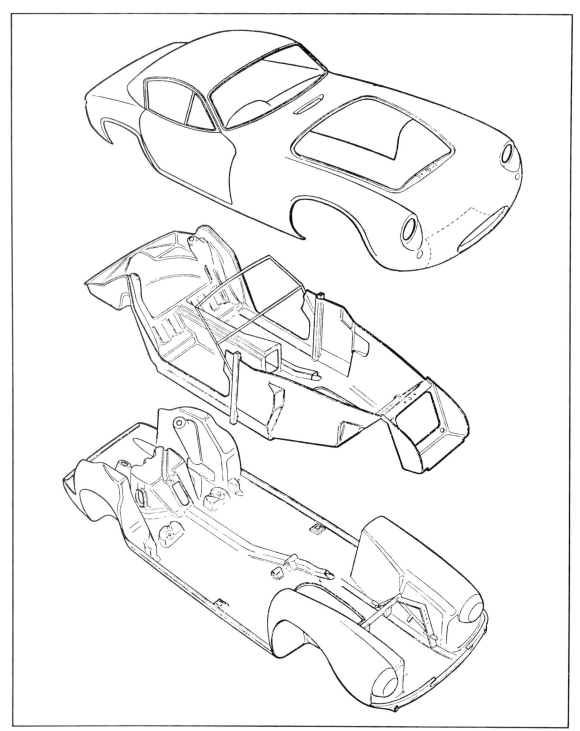

How a Lotus Elite is formed. All is fiberglass except for the steel front suspension frame and the windshield hoop. Costly at the time.

Chapter 4

Elan

In October 1962 Lotus announced an amazingly advanced new car, the Elan. Some say the Elan started as an 1100 cc replacement for the Seven, others say it was a convertible 1340 cc (Ford) replacement for the Elite. Either way, the car was a masterpiece.

While major, multinational automobile manufacturers spent millions on market research and prototypes to produce a new model that may gain an additional two percent of the market or maintain their share, Chapman would have similar ideas (usually arrived at in the bathtub), and then put his team to work on fiberglass and metal.

The original plan called for the new car to have a Ford four-cylinder engine and a chassis-less monocoque fiberglass bodyshell. However, the unexpected invention of the backbone chassis changed all that (explained in a later chapter). Suffice it to say that for 1962 a 1500 cc, twin-overhead-camshaft-powered car with twin 40 DCOE Weber carburetors, close-ratio gearbox, all-independent suspension, four-wheel disc brakes, pop-up headlights, glass side windows and a snug-fitting draft-free soft top were an amazing achievement.

The Lotus marketing people (me included) had to use the Elan as a major tool to hoist Lotus into a bigger, more profitable worldwide league of respected automobile manufacturers. Even while sales were high, plans were made to take the Lotus 26, the internal type number, up-market with a fixed-head coupe version featuring electric windows and carpeted interior.

At the same time, John Frayling was asked to redesign the car to include at least some

1963 Elan Drop Head shot in 1983 in Vancouver, Canada. At its simplest.

	Fun	Investment	Anguish
Lotus Elan	7	6	6
Lotus Elan Sprint Drop Head	8	9	3

Elan Drop Head Coupe and Elan fixed head coupe. Both bodies were made in the same mold. Registration suggests late 1965, early 1966.

A press shot suggesting how much luggage an Elan could accommodate. Where did the girl sit? Note chrome bumpers, circa 1965, and Dunlop SP41 tires. Were either fitted in production?

63

resemblance to the defunct Elite. He changed the trunk line, styled the roof section on Elite lines and cleaned up the interior. In 1965 the coupe emerged bearing type number 36, the drophead bearing type number 45, even though both bodyshells were formed in the same molds.

The original Elan saw two important improvements in its short life span. The S2 version featured a neater rear end treatment with six rear lights being replaced by a single cluster of lights on either side, improved weather equipment, locks to keep the sliding windows in the "up" position, stronger rubber "donuts" in the rear driveline, stronger connecting rods in the engine and larger brake calipers. Both the S1 and S2 were offered with an extra, detachable hardtop, but very few were ever supplied because of quality and distortion problems.

A Special Equipment version was offered with center-lock, peg-drive pressed-steel wheels fitted with Dunlop SP sport radial high-speed tires. A brake servo also came on this model, as did an optional center body stripe. The Special Equipment engine gave a reputed extra 10 hp (115 as opposed to 105) through revised camshafts, chokes, jets and spark advance/retard characteristics.

It has long been a Lotus policy to "massage" its sponsors by offering versions of the road cars in the livery of Grand Prix backers. This began in 1971, when the Elan appeared as the Sprint in Player's Gold Leaf colors (red, white and gold).

Lotus Elan coupe fitted with rare prototype chrome bumpers, believed not fitted in production. Clever registration digits pegged to the black grille individually.

When the American legislators, prodded by Ralph Nader, set about the task of making cars safer and pollution free, Lotus was the only British car builder to take the threat seriously. As a result only Lotus—out of the whole British motor industry—had cars to meet the requirements in 1966. In the years that followed, Gerry Doe, Lotus Legislation Compliance Engineer, traveled to and from Washington to ensure that Lotus cars always met the rules and regulations, marking a major turnabout for Chapman, who was always trying to find a way around the rules. Shortly after that, a dozen other countries jumped on the safety bandwagon and Doe's job became a nightmare, as they all had different requirements. Even in the face of this diversity, Lotus launched the Elan Super Safety. However, dealers asked the company to think of a different name, as it was rather conservative sounding for a sports car.

The Elan's original fiberglass bodyshell and immensely rigid steel-backbone chassis needed no alterations to meet safety requirements. Industry watchdogs, appearing more like vultures than engineers, were amazed at how well the Lotus held together in crash tests. In fact, the body was shipped home, repaired in less than forty-eight hours and went back on a development car!

The engine, however, needed a lot of detailed attention, including new Stromberg CD carburetors and revised spark advance/retard characteristics. Even after a grueling twenty-four-hour-per-day, seven-day-per-week 50,000 mile test on the Lotus circuit, the required certifications were achieved ahead of schedule. Meanwhile, other British manufacturers like Jaguar and MG were still saying, publicly at least, "They can't be serious can they?"

Both the coupe and drophead versions sold well in the United States and Canada, and at the same time benefited from the kit car tax concession in Britain. In order to meet steady market pressures and competition, the cars were upgraded in 1968 to Series 4 (S4) from the previous S3 model. The S4 had wider wheelwells to accommodate slightly larger tires, twin tail pipe mufflers, the rocker switch dash panel (required by

Day's of Cambridge, England, showroom, a modern dealer of classic cars. 1966 Drop Head on the left, a later Sprint on the right. Club Lotus England

the US government) and many minor changes that were aimed at saving Lotus money during production.

The Sprint model featuring the "big valve" engine was introduced shortly after the S4. The US version was fitted with modified Strombergs while Dell'Orto or Weber carburetors were fitted to the UK version. In 1971, claimed power output went up again and drivelines in US versions had to have special failsafe, flexible rubber donuts containing steel pegs that interlocked if the cou-

Lotus Elan Series 3; neat stowage of the soft top. Note fixed window frames. Club Lotus England

"Left hooker" in the United States in late 1967. Note changes from previous photograph. *Road & Track*

MODEL	Lotus Elan (Types 26, 36 and 45)
YEARS PRODUCED	1962-1974
BODY & CONFIGURATION	Front engine, rear drive. Open and coupe 2-seater sports in fiberglass. Separate rear luggage compartment. Electric window lifts from S3 model onward. Vacuum-operated pop-up headlights. Fully demountable body.
PURPOSE	Fast road use, not racing.
CHASSIS & SUSPENSION	Steel backbone chassis, bifurcated front and rear. Independent double-wishbone front with combined shock absorber and coil spring with antisway bar. Independent rear with Chapman strut.
ENGINE	1558 cc Lotus-Ford Twincam developing 105 bhp gross, initially, and uprated eventually to 120 bhp gross. Twin Weber, Dell'Orto or US-spec Stromberg CD carburetors.
TRANSMISSION	Lotus-Ford close-ratio or Ford semi-close ratio, all-synchromesh 4-speed. Hypoid-bevel final drive 3.9:1, 3.77:1 or 3.5:1. 4½J pressed-steel bolt-on or knock-off wheels. Disc brakes all round with optional servo.
NOTES	This car put Lotus firmly into profit and founded Chapman's multi-million-dollar fortune. Due to demand, the 26R racer was designed and built by Lotus Components Limited.

pling rubber failed. The last few of these cars featured an optional five-speed gearbox, the same unit that was offered on the Plus 2 and M.50 Elite. I don't believe any were shipped to the United States. Factory records show that no Federal Elan five-speeds were actually built—officially, that is.

The Lotus Elan line is divided historically and technically as follows:

Type 26: Elan known as the S1, S2 and Special Equipment S2

Type 26R: racing Elan and a later 26R/S2

Type 36: fixed head Elan coupe with newly styled trunk lines, integral hardtop, electric windows, carpet and so on

Type 45: drophead version of the coupe with the same features and built from the same mold

The 36 and 45 went on to an increased speci-

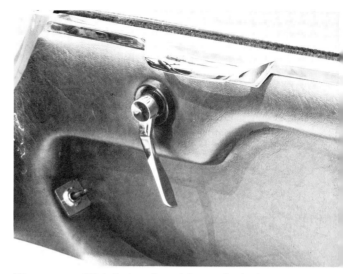

Elan coupe S3 interior door trim and window switch. Club Lotus England

The original Elan coupe on announcement day. The chrome bumpers were later to disappear, and before the exterior airflow vents were developed.

67

fication featuring the Big Valve Sprint package and the body in duo-tone paint.

It appears the "new generation" M 100 project from Lotus with the Toyota or GM powertrain will also carry the Elan name by 1988.

Elan changes

Date	Beginning chassis numbers	Change
October 1962	26/0001	Car introduced
January 1963	26/0026	Engine increased to 1558 cc
November 1964	26/3901	S2 introduced
September 1965	36/0001	S3 coupe introduced
January 1966	26/5282	Special Equipment model introduced
June 1966	26/26/5810	Last S2
June 1966	45/5702	First S3 drophead
March 1968	7895	S4 introduced Elan and coupe
November 1968	8600	Stromberg carburetors
December 1969	9824	Last of old numbering system
January 1970	7001.010001	New numbers
February 1971	7101 (?)	Big Valve Sprint introduced
February 1973	7302.0899	Last coupe Sprint

A suffix number appears after each chassis number: A, fixed head coupe; E, Special Equipment; C, drophead coupe; G, Special Equipment drophead; Q, export model. First two numbers of the new system denote year, second two denote month.

What to look for

Before you set out looking for an Elan, make sure you know the difference between the S1, S2 and better-equipped S3, S4 and Sprint later models.

Again, the biggest enemy of the chassis is rust. Take a good look at the front crossmember and suspension pick-up points. Also check for cracks around the engine mounts and differential tie rod attachment points. Beware of cars fitted with a roll cage, as they may have been used in competition.

The Elan's fiberglass body suffers the same deterioration as models already covered. Again look for crazing in the gel-coat,

Elan S4 coupe, 1968. Note all the changes. Were the spinners on the peg drive hub wheels illegal?

Elan Series 4 panel with safety rocker switches. Two knobs above the radio operate the hood release. Club Lotus England

Badge position and style. It speaks for itself.

Lotus Elan with optional hardtop, sold by Lenham Motor Company in Kent, England.

Stromberg CD carburetors without the federal emission cross-over pipes on the Lotus Elan. Club Lotus England

cracks in the fiberglass, poor-quality accident repairs, wide wheel openings and other custom additions.

Go over the engine and drivetrain thoroughly. Sometimes a previous owner may have replaced the original engine with a Ford, Alfa Romeo or Fiat engine because the proper repair or replacement was unavailable. Once you're sure you are looking at the right engine, check for excessive oil leaks, noisy, faulty or jamming starter motor and ring gear and a slack or leaking water pump. Look for cracked or broken differential mounting "ear pieces" and be wary of a noisy gearbox or one that jumps out of gear.

Make sure the dash panel and all instruments are in good working order; check the heater, defroster, pop-up headlights and electric window lifts. Notice if the seats are original and check that the soft top and tonneau cover are there and in good condition. Also make sure the windshield does not leak and is not cracked.

Driving impressions

Having driven an Elan across the United States and back again during the mid-1960s, I cannot only give my impressions but attest to the fact it is made for the United States. The Elan is very docile in street use unless,

Classic Series 4 Elan Stromberg. Note the "power bulge" to cover the taller CD carbs. This was even used when the UK cars reverted to Weber and Dell'Orto. Club Lotus England

of course, some fool has added wild camshafts. The car can be dropped into fourth gear at very low speeds but will still accelerate like a steam engine—especially earlier models with the 3.9:1 rear end ratio. However, the real advantage of the Elan is the handling.

"Handles like nothing else can—Lotus Elan" was the sales slogan in the late-60s, and it still holds true today. There is probably no other road car at any price that can out-handle an Elan. By *handling* I mean the ability to enter a sharp turn 25 mph too fast, brake down to cornering speed, accelerate out of the bend, swerve to avoid an old lady in a '48 Chevrolet, set the car up for the next bend and then screech to a halt because a tree has fallen across the road. Swervability equals safe handling in my book and a Lotus Elan has more of that than any other car.

By today's standards of automotive comfort it is not a quiet car but it is draft free. It only leaks in high-pressure car washes and can be driven thousands of miles without driver fatigue.

Decal on a very rare Elan five-speed. Perhaps only six were built but many more have been retrofitted with Lotus, ZF or Ford five-speeds. Club Lotus England

Finest of them all? 1972 Sprint Drop Head Coupe in gold leaf relief!

Autocrossing (or autotesting in the UK) is a popular sport for die-hard Lotus drivers and their valuable cars—not the hard knocks of circuit racing but using the car at its best; handling. One Elan is totally street, the other shows its rollbar as it spins out. Lotus Ltd, Maryland

The Elan concept lives on. The Christopher Neil Sports Cars Sprint Kit.

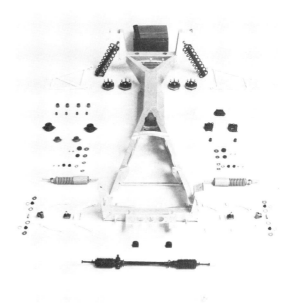

Christopher Neil Sprint Kit chassis and other components.

Actually a replica, circa 1985!

Nicely done Elan race car—typical of those raced in the late 1960s. Actually, 1986 at Laguna Seca. Tim Parker

Racing Elan, 1986 style. Max Payne's silhouette?

A wild one-off Elan built by a dentist. Basically an S2, circa 1964. Again, please don't. Actually a wider, shortened Plus 2 chassis.

The American version? A supercharged Elan in Los Angeles, 1981. Please don't. Club Lotus England

Chapter 5

Ford Cortina Lotus

Back in the early 1960s, the Ford Motor Company decided that a massive involvement in motor sports would turn the heads of prospective young car buyers (and they needed a boost after the Edsel fiasco). As a result Chapman was approached by Ford at Dearborn to go out and win the Indy 500, and by Ford of Britain to shoehorn a Lotus/Ford engine in the Ford of his choice. Chapman took a look at the Ford line, including the cars that were still on the "top secret" list, and chose the bland but lightweight Cortina bodyshell.

Using this as a base car he inserted the Lotus/Ford Twincam with its bottom end and gearbox matching the Elan's, a version of the Lotus Seven rear axle, and went to work on upgrading the front suspension incorporating 5½J wheels. Alloy doors, trunk and hood replaced the pressed-steel Ford pieces. Lotus was then contracted to build 1,000 of the cars—just enough to meet the required minimum to enter production-sedan races. Many of the cars were campaigned in the United States with great success both officially and privately.

When Ford introduced the Mk 2 Cortina, the fitting of engines and so forth was taken over by Ford and the cars (just) ceased to have quite the same appeal. The "works" Mk 2 car campaigned by Team Lotus for Jimmy Clark and other famous names used the Cosworth-designed Ford BDA sixteen-valve engine. I do not believe any of these cars survived to be sold into private hands.

Today the Mk 1 Cortina Lotus, with all the homologation equipment, is a very desirable collector car and ultracompetitive in

Lotus Cortina Series 1 engine bay. Very well restored. The engines used were identical to those in the Elan.

	Fun	*Investment*	*Anguish*
Ford Cortina Lotus	5	7	3

historic-sedan races. Later models of the Mk 1 reverted from A-bracket rear suspension to the standard Ford cart springs (and off came all the very vulnerable expensive alloy panels). The Mk 1 came in a white bodyshell with a pale green flash.

Ford Motor Company tells us that production figures were as follows:

Year	Number
1963	228
1964	536
1965	1112
1966	991
1967	1379 (includes the Mk 2 model with the new bodyshell)
1968	1484
1969	1036
1970	194

The Lotus factory offered two other versions of the Cortina Lotus sold directly to the customer. The first was the Special Equipment version with 115 bhp engine, Dunlop SP tires and adjustable rear shock absorbers. This package was dreamed up by Lotus Components Limited to help pay the rent (it cost an extra £124 and proved very popular). Lotus Components Limited also sold full race versions of the Cortina Lotus; approximately fifty of these were sold all over the world, especially to British Ford dealers from Los Angeles to Hong Kong.

The basic two-door Ford bodyshells, with some reinforcements and white finish, were delivered to Lotus from Dagenham. Lotus then put them on a separate production line where each car was fitted with the Lotus/Ford Twincam engine, close-ratio Lotus

Cortina Lotus Mk 1, 1963. I owned this former press car until it caught fire after an O-ring failure. Note console on the hood. Ford Motor Company

Road & Track used this photograph in its July 1964 issue. Are those cross-ply Dunlops fitted? A lot has happened in 20 years. *Road & Track*

gearbox, upgraded MacPherson strut front suspension, wider 5½J offset wheels, 165x13 tires and the modified Ford rear axle with its fragile A-bracket and coil-spring suspension.

Inside, the car received a distinctive dash panel with matching speedometer and tachometer, sumptuous seats and a wood-rimmed Lotus steering wheel with matching gearshift knob. The aluminum doors, trunk and hood were all supplied by Ford.

When assembly and road testing was complete, the distinctive green flash was added along with Lotus badges on the grille and rear fenders. The front quarter bumpers were styled from a small, contemporary Ford Anglia van. Of course, the grille was painted matte black since that was the fashion.

The Cortina GT built at Dagenham came in a full range of colors and could be ordered in two-door, four-door and even station wagon models. All models shared their brakes and front suspension setting with the Cortina Lotus, but the Lotus had a larger front antisway bar.

In Europe, many attempts have been made to convert GTs into Lotus forgeries. To detect such a forgery, look inside the trunk to see if the Lotus badge covers three holes (as drilled for the GT), or two (as drilled for the Lotus). Also check for two massive steel tubes coming up through the trunk floor to stiffen the rear suspension. One tube totally blocks off the spare wheelwell so that the wheel and tire are mounted on the trunk floor. The tubes were not fitted to all Mk 2s, however.

Next, examine the firewall under the hood for any sign of a cross-rod-operated throttle, as used on the Cortina GT's single double-choke Weber. The genuine Lotus has a cable-operated throttle. Documentation for the car should describe it as a Lotus Cortina,

MODEL	Ford Cortina Lotus (Type 28)
YEARS PRODUCED	Mk 1: 1962-1966; Mk 2: 1967-1970
BODY & CONFIGURATION	Pressed-steel unitary construction based on the production Mk 1 Ford Cortina, then Mk 2 bodyshell. Full 4-seater sedan with separate rear luggage compartment. Front engine, rear drive. Early models had alloy panels in doors, hood and trunk areas. Strengthening rods intrude into luggage and spare-wheel area.
PURPOSE	Fast road use with racing version. Homologation special.
CHASSIS & SUSPENSION	No separate chassis. Front suspension by MacPherson, strut and antisway bar. Rear suspension on first-series Mk 1s by solid axle and A-bracket with radius rods, coil springs and telescopic shock absorbers. Later Mk 1s and all Mk 2s had conventional Ford rear leaf springs.
ENGINE	Lotus-Ford 1558 cc Twincam producing 105 bhp. Lotus factory offered Special Equipment version with 115 bhp power output.
TRANSMISSION	Lotus-Ford close-ratio 4-speed all-synchromesh. 5½J bolt-on steel wheels. Disc front and drum rear brakes with servo as standard. Hypoid-bevel differential with 3.9:1 final drive.

Note the dash-end Airflow vents of this later Mk1 Cortina Lotus. Original steering wheels are now rare. Lotus Ltd, Maryland

"Boy racer" image was never better served than with the Mk1 Cortina Lotus in the late 1960s. Apart from the exterior mirrors this 1966 model looks good. Lotus Ltd, Maryland

or Ford Cortina Lotus or even Consul Cortina Sports Special Modified by Lotus. Of course it should have the Lotus/Ford Twincam engine. No four-door Cortina Lotus models or station wagons were ever produced.

The Mk 2 Cortina Lotus was built on Ford's assembly lines. The *only* difference between it and the GT was that the Lotus had a Lotus/Ford Twincam engine, still only available in a two-door. The Mk 2 was also available in every color on Ford's chart.

The Mk 2 is not quite as desirable as the Mk 1. The most collectible Mk 1s are those with the alloy panels and A-bracket suspension. This is because Ford quickly dropped these items to make the car nicer to drive, since several thousand had to be sold to the public to obtain the necessary homologations for racing. In the end over 2,500 Mk 1s were built. However, no reliable records can be found showing the total number of Mk 2s built, since Ford did not differentiate between them. There were 186 directly exported to the United States, and many proved almost impossible to sell until the works cars appeared at Sebring. Today there is a limited supply of body panels in the UK for the Mk 1 and Mk 2.

What to look for

When examining a Cortina, first verify its authenticity, then its engine and so on. Check the interior and exterior of all body panels for rust. Examine the front suspen-

Distinctive rear with those familiar Cortina taillights. Lotus badge looks later and "Lotus 28" (its type number) looks out of place, as do the back-up lights. Good, straight examples such as this are rare. Lotus Ltd, Maryland

sion closely, as it was canted backward for heavy braking which can distort the turret tops over the years. Also check for weak or leaking fuel lines and look for signs that indicate the car may have been used in competition.

Driving impressions

Most American drivers accustomed to ultrasoft suspensions and power steering with several thousand turns required lock-to-lock will find the Cortina Lotus a thoroughly unpleasant experience. It was designed for Europe's roads and tracks, and to be driven by European drivers.

Climbing high up into the heavily padded driver's seat, you will grasp a wood-rimmed steering wheel with a Lotus badge in the center. Straight ahead is a simple but highly informative instrument panel and a short hood (by US standards). Start the engine and you can hear every detonation while the gearshift lever starts to jiggle in sympathy. Interior noise is high, so don't buy an expensive stereo, and keep the speeds down if you wish to enjoy an exchange of intelligent conversation.

The four-speed Lotus/Ford close-ratio gearbox has one surprise in store: You can gun the engine up to a redline 6600 rpm before the rev limiter cuts in, giving an impressive 44 mph before a gear shift is required. Second and third are just as "long," and in fourth gear an indicated 115 mph is the most you will ever see—even with a strong tail wind.

Start to select first gear and the heavy clutch will suggest early left-leg fatigue. Turn the steering wheel and you will discover that half a turn creates a big and sudden change of direction with very little self-centering effect to bring the car back on line. In fact, some women owners, used to taking

A "works" Mk 2 Cortina Lotus with 16-valve BDA. Minilite alloy wheels lead a late-model Mk 1 (note changed grille and Cortina on the hood), also with alloy wheels, at Silverstone, England. Ford Motor Company

their hands off the wheel to let the car spin the wheel back, have performed dramatic U-turns.

Handling is certainly unusual; the car sits very high by modern standards and there is quite a lot of sway into turns. "I just lean against the door and keep my foot flat on the gas pedal," said the late Jim Clark when asked how he took one corner at Sebring. Despite the sway, the car handles very well indeed with that extra Lotus quality, "swervability." Anyone can design a suspension that will take a car around one curve really fast but it takes a Chapman to help you swerve from lock-to-lock to avoid an accident without creating your own. That's the fun of the Cortina Lotus.

The only fault in the handling is that you can't lift off suddenly when the car is cornering on the limit without inducing some nerve-tensioning changes of direction that take a Clark or a Moss to correct quickly and in a tidy manner. Graham Hill admitted that he could never master the technique of choosing just the right throttle opening for a given turn and then staying with it, right through the terror barrier. Chapman once took over the works car from ace English gentleman driver Jack Sears to show him the way around a fast turn at the Snetterton circuit. As the car rolled onto its roof, Chapman said, "That's how NOT to do it, Jack!"

UVX 565E is on this car, but is it the same Mk 2 as in the previous photograph? Generally, the later-shaped Cortinas don't have the charm of the early Mk 1s (and therefore the investment appeal?), but don't pass up a car like this one if it comes along. Ford Motor Company

Chapter 6

Elan Plus 2

Whenever a car manufacturer claims that an "all-new model is not a rehash of what went before it" or that the "new three-box design is not the hatchback with a trunk," it is usually lying. Similarly, when the Elan Plus 2 was launched, Lotus claimed it was not just a

The original Elan Plus 2 in a very royal setting, near Buckingham Palace in central London.

	Fun	Investment	Anguish
Lotus Elan Plus 2	6	5	5

stretched version of the base Elan. The car had Elan suspension, Elan brakes and Elan engine and transmission, but "oh no," it wasn't a stretched Elan.

We know, of course, that it was. The chassis was indeed stretched and widened. However, the bodyshell was really all new with the exception of the electric window lifts. The Elan Plus 2 was developed with great emphasis on aerodynamics. The car even shared wind-tunnel time with the Rover Turbine Le Mans car built by BRM, and the similarity is very obvious. On the other hand, similarity between the original, narrower prototype and the Opel GT has never been adequately explained.

The car was originally to be named Elite 2, but market research showed that the Elite Climax had such a bad reputation for reliability that any connection would have been counterproductive. The choice of the name Elan Plus 2 was based on the premise that satisfied Elan owners who now had families would see their future car within the ever-increasing range of Lotus cars.

Elan Plus 2 engine bay. Not all that much room. The servo to the left is no longer available as a spare part.

Developed in a wind tunnel for more than a year by Lotus, apparently alongside the Opel GT and the Rover-BRM gas turbine car.

The Plus 2 also pioneered double-curvature windows, achieved by cutting glass on the bias off a drum-shaped bed. The process was similar to cutting a section out of the central tube of a toilet roll, but at an angle to the center line. This enabled the glass to curve back with the shape of the car. Owners of Plus 2s know their cars are amazingly aerodynamic because, with the windows down, there is no draft. When cruising along a flat at 100 mph the car can be slipped into neutral with no noticeable deceleration for miles and miles—quite a spooky sensation.

The need to upgrade the cars for improved market acceptance and to hide cost and price increases resulted in the Plus 2S. This car featured the distinctive John Player black-and-gold paint scheme, and is now the fastest appreciating collector version of the Plus 2.

Hexagons of London was the first to convert these cars to convertible form in 1971. This is now done by Christopher Neil Sports Cars of Northwich, England, as part of a full restoration, which results in a general increase in rigidity. One station wagon version of the Plus 2 has been built privately, but there are no plans to go into production with it.

Elan Plus 2S. The two Lucas spotlamps under the bumper give easy identity. Club Lotus England

Plus 2 changes

Date	Beginning chassis numbers	Change
June 1967	05/0001	First Plus 2 chassis number
October 1968	50/1001	First Plus 2 luxury model
November 1968	50/1280	Stromberg CD carburetors fitted
January 1970	7001...L	New chassis number system
October 1970		Sprint Big Valve engine offered. Car now called Plus 2 130
January 1972		Optional 5-speed gearbox offered. Car now called Plus 2 130/5
December 1974	7402.1990L	Last chassis number

A Q suffix denotes export

What to look for

Since the Plus 2 was based on the original Elan, use the Elan check list when examining a Plus 2. Unfortunately, the changes in the body make for several more additions to the list.

Since the Plus 2 is wider and carries extra weight, the chassis and suspension are more susceptible to sagging, especially the rear suspension uprights. Also check the differential tie-rods and casing for cracks and broken mounts.

Watch for starter-jamming problems on models fitted with the five-speed gearbox, and noisy starters and ring gear on all other models. Also examine the five-speed unit closely for noises, cracks or malfunctions. While you're under the car, examine the gas tank closely for any signs of leaking. US versions had fail-safe pop-up headlamps, so if there is a vacuum leak, the lights will gradually creep up.

You may find a number of electrical problems affecting the ground, ignition, instruments and radio, but don't be overly concerned. There was an antitheft switch

On later Elan and Plus 2 models any systems failure in the headlamp vacuum causes them to rise, not drop. Club Lotus England

mounted in the glovebox, and its rather poor installation can be the source of all electrical malfunctions.

As you go over the exterior of the car you may notice dull or faded paint on the roof (this is common on later models with the metallic roof). All that is required is new paint. The rear bumpers are very difficult to replace, so look for damage. Also look for cracks in the gel-coat around the headlamps and check the Lotus alloy wheels for cracks, chips and corrosion. Also check the Twin-cam engine (discussed in detail elsewhere).

Driving impressions

This is really just a wide-track Elan and it feels like one. It also imparts a feeling of interior space. The Plus 2 is almost as well suited for street racing as the Elan, but just a bit less sensitive and responsive. This poses questions about the design abilities of the Detroit-based, so-called suspension and handling experts.

With a bigger cockpit and room for two children, the Plus 2 is also a quieter car than you would expect. No creaks, no rattles and the engine noise is well suppressed by the firewall and trunk area. The Plus 2 brakes are among the finest in any car, and that extra weight seems to make it slightly less nervous than its smaller brother.

Gear ratios are perfect for every use and that famous top-gear flexibility is the best

Lotus Elan Plus 2S federal interior, circa 1969. Club Lotus England

1982 factory entrance. Note sunroof on this Plus 2S, also peg drive wheels.

substitute for an automatic transmission that you could hope to have. No air conditioning was ever factory fitted, so in the best spirit of British colonial thinking, you just roll down the windows to keep cool. When the windows are down, you will appreciate the fine Lotus aerodynamics because you can't feel the air coming in and the car is just as quiet as with them up. For those who like to stay warm, the heater is from a very big British Ford four-door sedan (Chapman liked to have warm toes and a warm nose).

Lotus brand alloy wheels grace this Plus 2S. Their finish needs some looking after.

Chris Neil cabriolet conversion, which costs relatively little to do.

MODEL	Lotus Elan Plus 2 (Type 50)	**TRANSMISSION**	Lotus-Ford close-ratio or Ford semi-close-ratio all-synchromesh 4-speed. Austin Maxi 5-speed gear cluster with overdrive 5th gear in Lotus' own casing on the later Plus 2S/130/5-speed. 5J pressed-steel bolt-on or knock-off wheels with Lotus brand alloys on later S and 130 models. Rear axle ratios were 3.9 or 4.1:1; the higher 3.5:1 was not offered, being too high for the power and weight. Only one automatic car was built.
YEARS PRODUCED	1967-1974		
BODY & CONFIGURATION	Front engine, rear drive 2-plus-2 fixed head coupe in fiberglass with metal doorsill reinforcement. Separate rear luggage compartment. Electric windows. Vacuum-operated pop-up headlights. Fully demountable body.		
PURPOSE	Fast road use and family touring, not racing.		
CHASSIS & SUSPENSION	Steel backbone chassis, bifurcated front and rear, independent double-wishbone front suspension with combined coil and shock absorber with antisway bar. Independent rear with Chapman strut. Servo discs all round.	**NOTES**	This car had essentially a longer, wider Elan chassis with an all-new aerodynamic bodyshell to attack the family sports car market. From the basic Plus 2 it was made more of a luxury car with the higher specification Plus 2S followed by the 130 Big Valve cars and then the 5-speed version.
ENGINE	1558 cc Lotus-Ford Twincam 115 bhp Special Equipment version initially, then 120 bhp gross Big Valve, in later Plus 2S 130 models.		

Chapter 7

Europa

Ford's thunderous GT-40 coupes captured the imagination of sports car buffs like nothing since the MG TF. This is when Chapman penned the basic scheme for "the working man's GT-40," the Lotus Europa.

Gone forever was the roadster concept with the long hood, sweeping fenders and "wind in the hair" standards of weather protection as exemplified by the Lotus Seven. The sporting driver of the 1960s wanted ultrafast cornering, comfort and enough quiet to listen to a quality stereo/radio/cassette player in the car. It was equally important to be able to have an intimate conversation with a companion while cruising at 100 mph. While most owners did not have racing in mind they liked to see their choice of car confirmed by race winners (as was the Lotus 47 Europa racer).

Lotus Project Engineer Alan Jones took Chapman's early designs and, with the help of an outside design consultant, John Frayling, produced a set of drawings and a clay model for evaluation and wind-tunnel testing. Chapman was impressed.

While early designs were being produced, Chapman began a careful evaluation of available transaxles. At that time, Renault had quite an exciting range of new transaxles with five-speed options scheduled for early announcement. This was an ideal situation, as Chapman's original plan was to mate a Ford engine with a Renault gearbox. However, all this changed when Renault realized the PR potential of a link with Lotus, and subsidized the price of a complete engine/axle unit. Lotus took the engine and the big discount, and the Europa was born.

Renault had several similarly sized engines available but it is still not known for certain why this rare version of a Renault engine was chosen for the Europa. This particular engine was based on some components of the Renault 16, which was mostly used as a speed-boat engine for the US market.

Although the Renault PR department liked the idea of a Renault-powered Lotus, the Renault accountants did not; that is, not until they realized they were sitting with a large inventory of power-boat engines. So for Lotus to get the all-important transaxle, it also had to accept the engine. It turned out to be a sporty little unit, even if it did not have the more efficient cross-flow layout of the TS and TX engines which now find their way into old and tired Europas. When Lotus

	Fun	Investment	Anguish
Lotus Europa (Renault)	5	5	8
Lotus Europa Twincam	8	8	6

MODEL	Lotus Europa (Types 46 and 54)		producing approximately 80 bhp. Then 1558 cc Lotus-Ford Twincam in later Twincam and Special models producing 115 bhp in Special Equipment form and 120 bhp in Big Valve form in the Special.
YEARS PRODUCED	1967-1972		
BODY & CONFIGURATION	Mid-engine 2-seater GT coupe in fiberglass. Separate front and rear luggage compartments. Electric windows, fixed headlamps, brightmetal bumpers. Demountable bodyshell except on a few rare S1 models that also had fixed or semi-fixed windows.		
		TRANSMISSION	Renault 4-speed all-synchromesh transaxle, then Renault 5-speed transaxle in Special. 4½J bolt-on steel wheels with Lotus brand 5½J alloys on the Special. Disc front and drum rear brakes.
PURPOSE	Fast road use, not racing.		
CHASSIS & SUSPENSION	Steel backbone chassis, bifurcated front and rear, independent double-wishbone front suspension with combined coil spring and shock absorber units with antisway bar. Independent rear by wishbones and trailing arms. Rack and pinion steering.		
		NOTES	The main and immediate distinguishing feature between Renault and Twincam-powered models is that the side panels that obstruct rear-quarter vision were cut down on the Twincam and Special models.
ENGINE	Renault 1470 cc ohv all-alloy in S1 and S2		

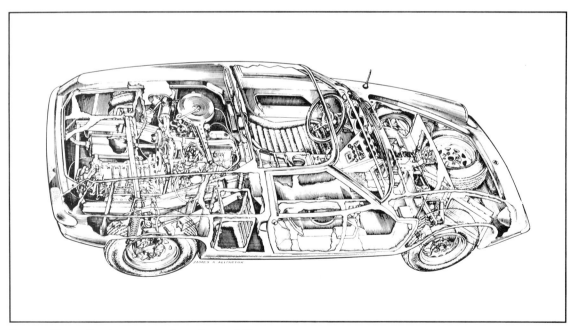

Europa Renault cutaway, courtesy James Allington. These cars are not as large as this view suggests. Club Lotus England

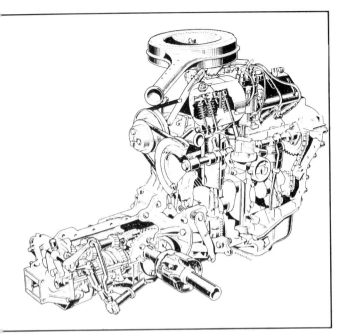

The Renault engine that Lotus bought for the Europa. Unkind comments abound, although it was fine when installed in the Renault 16 sedan.

first started talking to Renault, these more sophisticated engines were not shown to Chapman and did not enter into the negotiations.

Again, the engine choice was a bit of a surprise, especially when Chapman's plan called for the use of the maximum number of parts from existing Lotus cars plus the continuous use of proven design and construction techniques and materials. However, this instruction did give the car basic Elan front suspension, backbone chassis and fiberglass bodywork. Pop-up headlamps were eliminated.

For every million of Chapman's good ideas and obsessions, there was at least one mistake made on every new car. On the Europa he insisted on fixed windows, arguing that a good forced-air ventilation system made the others old fashioned and added an increased drag factor. Despite my objections that paying tolls, using drive-in banks and so on would be impossible, the S1 Europa came out with fixed windows. They were actually

The original Renault-engined Lotus Europa. The windshield sticker indicates its passing of the then-new Lotus quality-control scheme.

bonded in. For extra-good measure, the chassis was bonded to the bodyshell.

In a very short time Lotus was forced to make changes. Customer reaction caused the company to adopt an Elite (Climax) dropout window mechanism, followed by electric windows in the later S2. Insurance companies pointed out their reluctance to insure the cars if they would have to pay for a total loss or a new chassis and body after just a minor collision. So the Europa followed Elan practice and became a two-part car, rolling chassis and body.

An accomplished engineer, Mike Kimberley, joined Lotus from Jaguar and was immediately faced with a task that Lotus had said would never be done: to put the Lotus Twincam in the Europa, including a federal version.

This called for a new chassis, beefed-up suspension, improved gearshift linkage and a stronger gearbox with a five-speed option (still Renault). The body was slightly altered, as customer criticism of the rear-quarter visibility problem was met by cutting away the flying buttresses and smoothing the bodylines. In almost every other respect the car remained the same. Tire size was increased to 185x13 in the rear and 175x13 in the front. The optional Oatmeal interior proved to be popular.

This version was a success on the track, both in Britain and in the United States. Of course these cars were raced privately, as Chapman again ruled "no racing" as far as the factory was concerned. The most desirable cars are the five-speed Specials in JPS Team Lotus black and gold paint with the sharp Lotus brand GKN alloy wheels.

The racing version of the Europa Twincam was the Lotus 47, while the standard model and Twincam were type 54 and 74, respectively. As with the racing Elan, Chapman insisted that the car should be com-

American-specification (?) Europa, shot for *Road & Track*.

pletely re-engineered by Lotus Components Limited before being sold for pure racing.

In Lotus tradition, the works cars first raced at the annual Boxing Day Brands Hatch Christmastime meeting, and usually won first time out. In 1966, the Twincam type 47 came out five years ahead of the

The smooth lines of an early Renault-powered Europa. Note the air intakes over the engine bay. Club Lotus England

Europa chassis exposed during restoration. Cosmic wheels would be wrong for originality.

A beautiful five-speed Europa Special, 1974. Note the gold sill area. The last of an era. Club Lotus England

road-going Twincam (which Lotus swore it was never going to make, in order to maintain Elan sales).

The front suspension came from the Lotus 59 single-seater F3 and FB car, the front end was based on the Elan and Europa layout, with quicker rack-and-pinion steering, Rose joints replacing rubber bushes and so on. The drive shafts featured rubber couplings at the inboard ends and universal joints at the uprights.

Engines were usually Ford Cosworth 165 bhp dry sump Twincams with Tecalemit Jackson or Lotus fuel injection. Private owners preferred the Weber 45 DCOE for simplicity and reliability. The transaxle was by ZF and the wheels were cast-alloy, center-lock, peg-drive versions with various thirteen-inch options. The worst part of the design was the inadequacy of the brakes which persists today. Even the use of three-pot calipers and 10½ inch discs (versus the standard 9½ inch discs) did not help.

The bodyshell was still very much Europa, which gave very little access to suspension, engine, chassis and so on. Two 47s with Climax dohc engines were purchased by Team Elite to race at Le Mans but were unsuccessful.

US-specification (see side-marker lights) Twincam "Special S6" of 1974 at Arlington, Virginia. The gearshift mechanism is seen low and vulnerable. Lotus Ltd, Maryland

Europa Twincam. Note the cut-down rear quarters, the Lotus brand alloy wheels and the front spoiler.

Although homogated after fifty cars had been produced, less than forty have been traced in competition. The remainder were either sold as replacement bodyshells, used internally or fitted with pushrod or Twincam engines for street use. The factory used two shells as the basis for the Lotus 62 Europa which raced for the works with a prototype sixteen-valve two-liter engine, but these were probably not sold and eventually disappeared.

A Lotus 47 bears a chassis plate showing Lotus Components Limited as its origin. A Lotus Europa has a chassis plate showing Lotus Cars Limited, Norwich, Norfolk, or possibly just Lotus Cars Limited, Cheshunt, England. Lastly there was the one-off GKN 47D.

Europa changes

Date	Beginning chassis numbers	Change
May 1968	Prefix S2.	Renault engine, electric windows, separate chassis
December 1969	S2. 54/2950	Last model with this chassis numbering system
January 1970	7001.01000P	
January 1971	7001...	Continued production
October 1971	7105.12041P	Last S2
October 1971	7101...P	Twincam introduced
September 1971	72081783P	Special introduced
January 1973	7301.1969P	Twincam Special continued with optional 5-speed gearbox
November 1973	7311.2229P	European emission standard model
September 1975	7501.2434P	Final chassis number

A Q suffix denotes export

Few car manufacturers can claim so many constructors' titles, plus the Indy 500! Club Lotus England

The Europa Twincam cockpit layout was ergonomically superior to almost any other car in the mid-1970s. Steering wheel isn't stock. Club Lotus England

The tasteful interior of a late-model Europa Twincam. Known as the color Oatmeal, it was inclined to get very dirty, and proved hard to clean. Club Lotus England

What to look for

If you have decided that you want to buy a Europa, talk with or correspond with owners before you look for "your" car. A few weeks of ownership will tell more of what you want to know about the car than an entire book will. These cars have had their fair share of problems, and the extent will differ from car to car. The general rules apply for examining a Europa: Look for straightness, rust, cracking, rippling and poor-quality repairs. The price will come down as you find more problems. Too bad you won't find them all.

Driving impressions

The first order of business is learning how to get into the thing: Fully extend your right leg (as if you were getting into a wet suit) and place it well to the right of the throttle. Now roll into the car, leaning on the seat as you transfer your body weight from your left leg on the curb to your right leg on the car floor. (There is no need to put your hand in the puddle as you get in.) If this is your first drive in a Europa, you will undoubtedly turn blue from claustrophobia when you shut the door.

There you sit with unobstructed vision out the front and sides. However, the back-view is like looking through a mail slot. There is absolutely no visibility at the rear corners. Before firing up the engine, you may want to grab some ear plugs, especially on the early Renault-powered models. This is because the genius-inspired backbone chassis is also a tuning fork and picks up every vibration, magnifying it twenty times. Things get better once you speed up. (I have it on good authority that once past the sound barrier the noise completely goes away.)

The rear ratios are spaced well, and right

What a Europa Twincam will look like if somebody steals the body in the night! Gearbox casing is a work of art.

Front luggage space in the Europa. Club Lotus England

where they need to be for fast point-to-point driving. Gear selection will be smooth and crisp if the linkage has been well maintained, or vague and sloppy if the joints have been neglected or the engine mounts have become soft from leaking oil.

Steering is ultradirect and very responsive, and the handling is pure Lotus—especially on dry roads. The soft ride and zero body roll invite you to go into every curve as fast as you dare and come out of it with a big smile. There is a slight understeer toward neutral as the power comes on, making it nearly impossible to swing the back end out in a curve unless the road is wet. Beware, the Europa is a real handful on a wet curve for the inexperienced driver. Learn what the car is telling you before you have to tell it to the insurance adjuster.

The all-conquering Chris Meek, racing the Europa that won more races than any other Lotus car in history.

Engine bay of works 47. Note fuel injection and alternator position. Lotus Ltd, Maryland

Note side filler and alloy center lock wheels on this Lotus 47 racer. Windows are fixed. Club Lotus England

47 at auction in Monterey, California. Needed a lot of work but it could have made it. Tim Parker

The GKN 47D one-off was powered by the Buick-based Rover V-8 and is still exhibited today by the GKN Engineering Group in Britain. Club Lotus England

A rare special-bodied GS Europa. An alternative solution to the rear-quarter vision problem.

Chapter 8

Elite and Eclat (Sprint)

When the Lotus Elite was launched in the United States the dealers and the public did not like its lines. "Looks like a Gremlin somebody trod on" said one previously enthusiastic dealer. The cut-off, station wagon look had been pioneered by Reliant, another British specialist manufacturer. However, the success of its top-selling Scimitar had not reached the United States.

So the message was flashed back to Hethel: "Put a conventional rear end on the car and it will sell." Lotus stylist Oliver Winterbottom went to work on several ideas, and a conventional tail design was finally agreed upon. To rush the car into production Lotus reverted to hand layup molds which produced a lighter bodyshell, making the new rear end much lighter than the Elite's.

The prototype was shown to American dealers and orders came in fast, but they would not accept the name Eclat. "Isn't that a Danish pastry or some type of disease?" quipped one dealer. So Sprint became the car's name. (The importers also vetoed the wheels as "too bland.")

There is an anecdotal story about a proud new owner of an Elite who opened the rear hatch and threw his golf clubs in head first. They bounced back out again, but not before they had shattered the noise-insulating second rear glass between the luggage area and rear passenger compartment.

The Elite and Eclat (Sprint) feature the classic Lotus inverted-U steel-backbone chas-

MODEL	Lotus Elite (Type 75)
YEARS PRODUCED	1974-1983/84
BODY & CONFIGURATION	Front engine, rear drive, 4-seater, 2-door coupe with "hatch" trunk. Vacuum injection molded in fiberglass. Air conditioning available. Body fully demountable.
PURPOSE	Fast family motoring.
CHASSIS & SUSPENSION	As Eclat.
ENGINE	As Eclat.
TRANSMISSION	2-liter models have Austin/Lotus 5-speed all-synchromesh. 2.2-liter models have Getrag 5-speed all-synchromesh. Borg-Warner automatic also available.
NOTES	A very few Elite Riviera models were made before the car was phased out.

	Fun	*Investment*	*Anguish*
Lotus Elite and Eclat (Sprint)	6	4	9

Series 1 Elite—launch time? The belt line clearly shows the two bodyshell halves, top and bottom.

Lotus Elite, 1977, Series 1. These are the cars with the rust-prone chassis.

sis with all-independent suspension. The factory took a step backward, however, by fitting inboard rear drum brakes to get a lower unsprung weight and legal handbrake performance. The traditional vacuum-operated, fail-safe headlamps were retained along with the wide-opening doors and plenty of leg and head room. For the first time, factory air conditioning, power steering and a three-speed automatic transmission were offered on a Lotus.

The automatic gearbox, a Borg-Warner 45, was "Tuned by Lotus" to better suit the famous Lotus 907 engine. This engine was based on the unit fitted to the Jensen-Healey and made the Lotus capable of 130 mph. The manual transmission was the Lotus/British Leyland five-speed gearbox first seen in the Plus 2 S130 five-speed and a few Elans. Final drive was through a beefy Salisbury crown-wheel and pinion thought to be common to an earlier Jaguar model.

Although the outstanding Lotus 907 engine is dimensionally similar to the 2.3 liter slant-4 Vauxhall/GM engine, it is pure Lotus and not a Vauxhall. In the mid-1960s Chapman took a close look at the tightening noose of US legislation aimed at reducing air pollution, and realized its proponents were serious and determined. He knew that hanging air pumps and other power-robbing devices on an engine was not the way to go, so he started drafting plans for a highly efficient new engine.

Ron Burr, recruited from Coventry Climax, and Chapman set out to design a V-8 and slant-4 that was to be "a Japanese copy of the Cosworth DFV head and combustion chamber" as Chapman put it. The idea behind designing two motors was to get a low hoodline for the production cars as well as an engine for a 100 percent Lotus effort at Indianapolis.

As Burr and the Lotus team were working on the new engine, GM/Vauxhall was also working on a new slant-4 project. In 1967, Chapman saw this new powerplant at the London Motor Show sporting a block and crank that nearly matched the proposed new Lotus unit. The Lotus engine was then re-

US dealers see the Elite for the first time and despite Martini-inspired smiles they voted it down for its unusual rear-end styling. "Looks like a Gremlin that somebody trod on!" said one. Lotus MD Mike Kimberley (with striped shirt) with co-director Roger Putnam on his left.

drawn so the GM block and crank could be used for testing, which would shorten development time by almost a year. The all-alloy block and Lotus crank soon followed.

Preproduction engines were fitted to Vauxhall cars for testing under all conditions—even in a panel van. Racing engines were also prepared for Lotus 62, Europa team cars and the Texaco Star Formula 2 debacle. Chapman's desire was to build a two-liter engine. I argued long and hard to produce initially a 1.8 liter version with the capacity to go to 2.4 liters as the market demanded. "We can bury price increases in new models with bigger engines, and with only 1.8 liters we can see how we get on with transmission warranty claims before pushing up the torque and horsepower," I argued.

Chapman would have nothing to do with it and thumped the table saying that it would be two liters, nothing more and nothing less—*ever*. Several years later the company had to invest a vast sum of money and time into getting the motor up to 2.2 liters for the Chrysler/Talbot Sunbeam Lotus sedan as well as the 2.2 liter version of the Elite, Eclat (Sprint) and Esprit.

A major feature of these engines was the US Royal toothed-belt system for actuating the valve gear, which was far ahead of most competitors. Unfortunately, however, the early engines did not have belt tensioners, which resulted in some disastrous engine failures. This usually happened in cold weather as the alloy engine contracted and the belt became rigid.

Aerodynamics received a lot of attention, as the wedge shape suggests. The Elite bodyshell was made by the new Lotus patented VARI process (Vacuum Assisted Resin Injection) developed jointly with Scott Barder Limited. Many thousands of test miles went into the car before its debut, but despite this thorough preparation, the early cars were probably more unreliable than any previous Lotus. This caused dealers to turn their backs on the mobile warranty claims.

People often ask me why Chapman deserted all his existing customers in the sports car business and jumped up-market to a whole new line of cars that did not represent a logical upward progression, either in price or specification. With the stroke of a pen, the air-in-the-hair dropheads and sports coupes were written out. Was this an act of folly or grand design?

Once another oil crisis had threatened paralysis to motorists and death to the gas guzzlers, Lotus people could be heard claiming their new generation of aerodynamic models with fuel-efficient, low-pollution engines proved what forward thinkers they

Series 2 Elite 2.2 liter. Not shipped directly to United States. Check the changes with the side-profile Series 1.

Lotus production line at Hethel in the late 1970s.

were. That made a great press release, but it was far from the truth.

Ford had advised Lotus that blocks for the 1600 Twincam would soon be unavailable. A tall-block alternative would not work since the head was already at the limit of its breathing space and could not handle anything over 1800 cc. The head was also very expensive to machine and could not be produced on the modern computerized machines. So the 907 engine was designed to meet all requirements, including lower production costs and ease of assembly.

All three existing cars, Elan, Plus 2 and Europa, could not possibly comply with impending US regulations, and a new form of tax in Britain outlawed the "kit car" version of Lotus cars and automatically increased prices by fifteen percent. Therefore the cars were on their way out.

Chapman's big mistake was to merely accept the new US regulations and not tell his lieutenants to "cross the pond and get some easement for the Elan and Europa." He argued that it was better financially to sell 500 cars at a $1,000,000 profit than to sell 2,000 cars and achieve the same end. Especially when sales of 500 cars meant 500 warranties; 2,000 cars spelled a much greater contingent liability situation, not to mention aggravation. Finally, Chapman was bored with the existing cars and sought some excitement.

What to look for

So what of today's used Elite and Sprint? Your first probe must be the rear-end chassis bridge between the suspension uprights. These simply rust away to dust, and that

1980 Lotus Elite/Eclat Series 2.2. Note interior roof beam.

The very rare Elite Riviera 2.2 liter that was never exported. Very collectible! Club Lotus England

A shipment for the United States, circa 1976. One car has its headlamp up (?). Apparently these cars arrived frozen solid because no one remembered the anti-freeze in the mild English October.

Series 1 Eclat sold as Sprint in the United States.

means a new chassis. The later, galvanized-chassis cars didn't find their way directly to North America via importers.

The Lotus gearbox (not the Getrag) is a very weak point and should be check thoroughly. The actual internals come from a British Austin Maxi but Lotus had something to do with honing them to make them quieter when installed in the Lotus alloy casing. So listen for doom-predicting noises and watch for prematurely worn clutch, cracks and oil leaks.

The engine should be quiet, whether hot or cold, with no rumbles coming from the bottom end. Beware of worn timing gears. What sounds like a terminal engine rattle at 3500 rpm is probably just the fiberglass safety shroud over the toothed timing belt (one or more bolts have been known to come loose and allow the cover to vibrate). Also check for oil leaks around the cam covers and exhaust headers. Cam covers are very lightly torqued but owners will try to stop oil leaks with a long-handled wrench.

The water pump is very expensive to replace, so inspect it carefully. On early cars, as well as the Esprit, the water pump was not strong enough to keep the water circulating to keep the car and driver cool at the tickover. The fans were frequently overridden by zealous home mechanics who installed a switch in the cockpit. See that the fans are operative. The vulnerable front airdam was also a vital part of the cooling system, but most cars lost their "shovel" due to low clearance. They were probably not replaced

MODEL	Lotus Eclat (Sprint) and Excel
YEARS PRODUCED	1976-
BODY & CONFIGURATION	Front engine, rear drive, 2-Plus-2 2-door coupe with rear luggage trunk. Fiberglass construction. Air conditioning available. Body fully demountable.
PURPOSE	Fast family motoring.
CHASSIS & SUSPENSION	Steel backbone chassis, bifurcated front and rear. Double-wishbone front suspension with combined coil spring and shock absorber. Rear suspension trailing arm, lower transverse link, and fixed-length drive shafts. Rack and pinion steering with power option wheels alloy, 14-inch 7J section. Disc front and drum rear brakes with servo.
ENGINE	Lotus 2-liter 907 then 2.2-liter 912, 16-valve belt-driven dohc. All-alloy slant-4-cylinder engine with Twin Dell'Orto or Stromberg carburetors. 145-180 bhp.
TRANSMISSION	2-liter models have Austin/Lotus 5-speed all-synchromesh. 2.2-liter has Getrag 5-speed, all-synchromesh. Excel has Toyota 5-speed, all-synchromesh. Optional Borg-Warner automatic.
NOTES	Starting life in the UK as "Eclat," the car was called "Sprint" in the US. The British use of this name came later. Some 2.2 models featured sunroof and got the name "Riviera." Now the car is "Excel" or "Excel SE."

Eclat (Sprint) interior, 1978-79. The seat cloth has proven almost impossible to clean.

because the owners were quoted horrendous prices for replacements.

The front suspension is also a weak point, so check for seized or stiff trunnions. While you're under there, look the frame over for major rust, distortion and damage. Other weak points are rear wheel bearings, rear drive shaft universal joints and even the rear lower longitudinal bolts which creak when dry and sometimes break "in situ."

Closely examine the windshield wiper motor, especially for signs of overheating. It seems Lotus suspended the wiper motor gearbox from the ceiling and built the car around it! The labor charge for replacement is unbelievably high. While inside, check the air conditioning, pop-up headlamps, door locks and hinges.

Driving impressions

A first impression of the Elite in the United States is its funny shape. In Europe it is better appreciated; however, once in the driver's seat, that all fades away. The five-speed gearbox (Lotus on early models then German Getrag) is notchy but nice, with a gear for every situation and every emergency. There is even a three-speed automatic version.

The Elite certainly took Lotus up-market in a hurry. Power steering, air conditioning, electric windows and capacity for four adults packed in aerodynamic splendor and propelled to 130 mph by the Lotus two-liter, sixteen-valve, twin overhead cam engine.

The car handles in true Lotus fashion, even fully loaded. Get into a turn fast, dab

Lotus Eclat (Sprint) and one of Chapman's luxury yacht designs that was due to be sold in the United States by Chris-Craft.

the brakes at the apex and power out with the flick of the wrist to bring an errant tail back in line. Soar up and down the gearbox for fun, even in the wet. Cruise at legal speeds and carry on normal conversation or savor the stereo. It is all here in the fabulous Elite.

As for the Eclat (Sprint), it is a little noisier and the rear springs are too hard, as they were selected for the tail-heavy Elite.

Eclat (Sprint), 1978. Ugly badge on the left.

The latest version of the Eclat (Sprint) is the Excel S/E, 1986—with an extra 20 bhp.

Lotus Eclat Series 2.2. 1981 model year.

The rare Eclat Riviera sold only in Britain during 1982-83. Some prefer it to the Excel. Very collectible.

1986 Lotus Excel S/E. Fresh wheels and even lower profile tires, these are from Goodyear. Note the new badge on the hood.

1986 Lotus Excel S/E. Giugiaro-designed steering wheel is appropriate.

1986 Lotus Excel. Into the lap of luxury, for those with short legs. Leather is now an option for the cloth used here.

Chapter 9

Esprit

Chapman had absolutely no plans to replace the Europa when he went to the Turin Auto Show. There he saw a Giorgetto Giugiaro Ital Design styling exercise on a Europa chassis, and the wheels in his genius mind began to turn. Lotus bought the car and re-engineered it to house the 907 two-liter powerplant. The result was the first "Ketteringham Hall Special," which ironically was not produced in Lotus Developments and which led to a little "That's your problem" attitude later.

During the development stages of the car, Lotus in-house stylist Oliver Winterbottom resided in Turin to mastermind the design with the Italians. In 1975 Lotus Esprit made its debut at the Paris Show. It was a real show stopper, and its appearance hard on the heels of the Elite and Eclat was a sign of a dramatic surge toward growth for Lotus.

The show and press cars were loaded with an unbelievable number of special modifications and unique methods for cutting down resonance from the wishbone (or tuning-fork) chassis. This even included double glazing the small rear window between the cockpit and the rear trunk/engine compartment. If you were paid to drive an early model Esprit, the law would require you to wear ear defenders, as also required in a tractor cab. All of these early models were subject to a semiconfidential recall, which was an understatement. Some of the modifications were unbelievable, if not horrific, in their implications, but no worse than those of other much larger and wiser car builders.

Lotus Developments was now forced to come up with a Mk 2 as quickly as possible. During this process many of the major defects were corrected, including a decent cooling system. The engine had such a marginal cooling system that Mobil SHC synthetic oil had to be specified to preserve the engine. Early cars had Otto temperature-sensing switches which literally blew out from overheating pressure. To remedy this, Lotus did the only obvious thing and wired them in like champagne corks. Now if they blow they really fly.

Other cars had the problem of gasoline spraying all over the coil until the engine stopped. Once the gas dried off you could start again—until the problem recurred or the car caught fire. There was also a problem with low air pressure under the engine cover, which meant no air circulation but

	Fun	*Investment*	*Anguish*
Lotus Esprit S1 and S2	6	5	9
Lotus Esprit S3 and Turbo	8	7	5

plenty of heat and built-up road grime. This produced a grimy engine covered in gasoline that overheated and stopped running in rain. Many owners relocated the coil in the rear where it was cool and dry.

Enormous effort was put into the Esprit under the leadership of Mike Kimberley. As a result, the S2 and S2/2.2 were much better cars. Meanwhile, the company was working on even better cars, namely the S3 and the Turbo.

The S3 was a totally re-engineered car in comparison to its predecessors, but this advanced engineering was even further enhanced by the Lotus Esprit Turbo. During the early stages, the entire world of turbocharging was scrutinized and summarized under Chapman's close attention. Lotus Developments bought a wide range of turbocharged cars and looked at every kind of turbo unit, from Chapman's airplane to prewar superchargers to Saab turbos. They drove them and then stripped them to gain knowledge and expertise in the state-of-the-art. Every shortcoming was noted as the Lotus Turbo project had to ensure the Turbo Esprit would be a problem-free unit from the start.

As this development work was going on, both Winterbottom and Giugiaro were busy redesigning the car. They were asked to "tidy up" the styling, and the final version showed the influence of both men. The new front bumper had an integral and deeper spoiler along with pronounced sideskirts. NACA ducts fed air to the engine and turbocharger, and the rear deck had a more pronounced lip to aid downforce at high speed. The rear window gave way to a slatted aperture that was good for visibility and cooling. The last real visual difference was a small skirt under the tail.

The engine that finally went into the new Esprit was known as the Type 910. It was fitted with a Garret AiResearch turbocharger, pumping 8 psi through twin Dell 'Orto

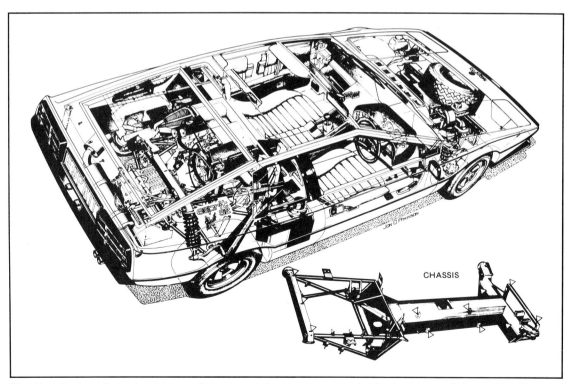

The Esprit chassis and cutaway of the general layout of an S2 Esprit. Certain general principles are similar to those of the earlier Europa. Note the spaceframe engine bay.

The original Esprit S1. Simple, unadorned and exactly as the designer wanted it to look.

The first batch of US-specification Esprits being built in 1977. The quality wasn't good enough for the critical American market.

Final work on an Esprit bodyshell at the Lotus factory. Replacement shells or sections are readily available.

carburetors. Compression was reduced to 7.5:1 and a different camshaft was used to better suit the characteristics of the engine and to optimize torque output. The whole engine was re-engineered for longer life and greater torsional rigidity and durability. Power output went from 150 bhp to over 210 at 6250 rpm and maximum torque was at 4500 rpm.

When the cars first appeared, they received rave reviews from the press but the early warranty problems were dealt with in strict secrecy by tight-lipped employees behind closed doors. Rumors spread of blown engines and such, but these were largely unsubstantiated and probably arose out of the secrecy.

To commemorate the 1979 Lotus World Championship a limited number of Esprits were built with the year encircled in laurel leaves on the rear quarter. By the time these cars were available, Lotus had gone over to

The famous "007" car that appeared with James Bond in *The Spy Who Loved Me.*

Martini sponsorship and green cars, so Martini Team Green was also added to the color chart. With Essex taking a strong position in Lotus sponsorship the first Esprit Turbos featured the metallic blue and silver of Essex. This arrangement ended as soon as sponsorship switched back to JPS.

The very early models in the Essex livery had dry-sump engines, but they were dropped with the last Essex models. If you are looking at an Essex Esprit make sure you have the car's complete service history and check to see that the engine number is the same as on the documentation.

As the engine was revised, the chassis and suspension were also subject to revision. First, the new chassis was galvanized to eliminate the anticipated long-term rust problem that had manifested itself in all other Lotus backbone-chassis cars. The rear engine bay and suspension pick-up zones were totally redesigned to stop noise and vibration buildup. This was a big problem in the S1 and S2 Esprits, and Chapman wanted the problem "designed out" of the new models.

The front and rear suspensions were redesigned in some detail, especially at the rear where the drive shaft was no longer a part of the suspension. (This also gave the drive shafts a lot more durability.)

Only a one-inch increase in clutch diameter was needed to take the extra power, and the swept area of the disc brakes was also increased slightly. Those close to the project also knew that the revised chassis would accommodate the proposed Lotus V-8 in years to come.

The dramatic scramble to buy the American federal version of the Esprit took the company totally by surprise. Early customers even paid a premium to have their cars flown to California. Unfortunately, a Lotus "technical trouble-shooter" had to be on the next plane as trouble brewed.

Esprit Series 2 interior. This is the Marcasite material (imitation suede) that bleaches in the sun! Club Lotus England

Series 2 Esprit with modified styling, and improved cooling. Club Lotus England

One of the biggest problems was, again, overheating. The engines were tuned to idle at 650 rpm, which did not turn the water pump fast enough. Good dealer preparation remedied this—the car was set to idle at 1100 rpm to keep the car cooler in traffic. Many of the other problems were associated with poor dealer preparation. A small but significant epidemic of warped cylinder heads resulted from "cooked" engines, as Otto switches blew out due to faulty installation.

As US sales of the Esprit took off, Lotus introduced subtle changes that stole two inches of leg room and as much again in head room. For the taller driver, Lotus even offered a removable glass top. Perhaps the six-foot-four-inch Mike Kimberley, Lotus managing director, had something to do with the larger accommodations. Previous cars had been designed to fit Chapman's shorter stature.

Recent Lotus dealer reports in the United States say that the Esprit Turbo is proving more than adequately reliable, and its engine even keeps cool. A leading dealer said the biggest problem is that owners won't leave the engine alone.

Only recently have Esprits appeared in serious racing form. During 1983 and 1984 the Esprit S3 and Turbo were raced with some success. The factory has not built any racing or competition cars—so far. "Funny cars" using Esprit look-alike bodies covering pure racing spaceframe chassis and a wide variety of engines have been around for some time but they are not true Esprits, so beware.

What to look for

One of the first things to verify when examining an Esprit is that it is not a Series 1 dressed up to look like a Series 2. This is easily done by fitting a later type of spoiler. The extra cooling ducts and trunking in and to the engine bay cannot be added, however. Check the backside of the body panels for accident repairs or fiberglass surgery.

Inspect the entire chassis for rust. Focus especially on the front cross-member section and in the tubular rear area around the engine and where the tubes meet the backbone.

The engine should run quietly with oil pressure between forty and sixty pounds and stay cool even in a Dallas traffic jam in

Series 3 Esprit (without the Turbo). The fine lines of the original car are gone but build quality is vastly improved.

The original Bell & Colvill Turbo Esprit that started a trend. Club Lotus England

Lotus Turbo Esprit, the official answer. Compare the detail styling with the S3.

mid-summer. If not, check that the thermostatically controlled heater fans are working (some cars had up to three). Also see that the heater works.

The gearboxes, crownwheel and pinion, and clutches on the Esprit are not the most durable components, especially in drag-style traffic-light starts. Ensure that clutch and gear changes are smooth and unbalked and that there is no obvious noise in any gear. Also check that all gears stay firmly in place when you lift your foot off the gas pedal.

It is essential to check tire type and condition, as replacements are far from cheap.

MODEL	Lotus Esprit
YEARS PRODUCED	1976-
BODY & CONFIGURATION	Mid-engine, 2-seater fiberglass coupe with luggage space front and rear. Optional removable roof panel in later models.
PURPOSE	Fast road use.
CHASSIS & SUSPENSION	Pressed-steel backbone chassis with tubular-steel spaceframe engine bay. Independent double-wishbone front on S1. Independent rear with semi-trailing arm and transverse link. Independent with upper wishbone plus lower transverse link. Unequal-length transverse links and radius arms on S2 onward.
ENGINE	Lotus 16V dohc. Belt-driven all-alloy slant-4 2-liter. 2.2 liter or turbo producing 145-210 bhp. Dell'Orto or Stromberg carburetors. Fuel injection on 1987 model Turbo.
TRANSMISSION	Citroen 5-speed all-synchromesh rear-mounted gearbox/transaxle, 4.37:1 ratio. S1 had 14-inch wheels; 6-inch front, 7-inch rear. S2 onward, 7J/15 front, 8J/15 rear. Servo discs all round.
NOTES	Later chassis after circa 1982 are galvanized.

Driving impressions

To get an idea of what this cockpit is like, go back and read about the Europa—this one is worse, on both counts.

The Esprit is based on the Europa but with a bigger engine to make more noise and vibration. Handling on the earlier S1 and S2 models was not up to Europa or even, some say, Lotus standards. But by rejecting Doctor Porsche's idea of hanging the engine out back where only luggage and muffler pipes belong, it can outrun any Porsche.

Gear linkage was never a strong feature of earlier cars. If it was poorly maintained, shifting can be a combination of guesswork and muscles. You'll find the brakes are just fine, after you get used to their width. Keep an eye on the coolant temperature, as earlier cars were known to overheat in summer weather with some disastrous effects.

Luggage room is greater front and rear than the Europa but you will have to get used to warm underpants and hot toothpaste because the luggage compartment sits over the engine and muffler. All this aside, the Esprit is a very satisfying car to drive in almost every respect, especially the latest Turbo.

US-specification Esprit Turbo in Essex Petroleum colors. BBS-style wheels were popular. This shot shows the difference in rim width, front to rear. Lotus Ltd, Maryland

Terry Kite, winner of the Club Lotus Trophy in 1985, at Silverstone. Car is virtually stock.

This American-specification 1983 Esprit Turbo was purchased in October of that year by owner C.P. Traver.

Same molds, different trimmings. An early S1 Esprit and the latest Turbo model with Federal bumpers and full-width air dam.

1986-model Esprit Turbo awaiting a buyer. Interest is waning, as seen in this photograph. Club Lotus England

A lightweight bodyshell for this car was supplied out of the factory back door. Insufficient braking power apparently inhibited wins, despite 250 bhp Vegantune engine with original downdraught Lotus cylinder head.

Esprit Turbo convertible, believed to be a one-off, came from Kollinger in West Germany. The photo was shot at Silverstone during the 1984 British GP; a Lotus 16 is alongside. Lotus Ltd, Maryland

Chapter 10

Chrysler/Talbot Sunbeam

The Sunbeam Lotus never reached the US market. The car was a joint project between Lotus and Chrysler Europe through the British-based subsidiary, the home of the old Sunbeam Tiger.

Part way through the production run Chrysler sold the company to Peugeot of France. They named them Talbots, but the line was not dropped immediately.

The Cortina Lotus formula was applied to this very light, subcompact Sunbeam sedan (the bodyshell was essentially the same design as the Plymouth Horizon/Dodge Omni, but rear drive) and a 2.2 liter, sixteen-valve Lotus engine mated with the rugged five-speed ZF gearbox was installed. With suitable upgraded brakes, suspension, pick-up points and tires, this car was a sure-fire winner on the international rally circuits. It met all its expectations and must go down in automotive history as one of the most exhilarating sedans ever built. Both the Cortina Lotus and the Sunbeam Lotus were chosen by British police forces for marked and unmarked traffic patrol cars.

I had one for almost twelve months and would have kept it if the roadholding had equaled the engine power and its owner's erratic driving style. These cars were never officially raced in Europe.

A later project, named Horizon, called for the Esprit Turbo's 2.2 liter engine to be fitted in a smaller bodyshell but was canceled by the new owners of the company. They preferred to build what became a very successful mid-engined rally car in the Renault R5 concept using four-wheel drive. They called it a Peugeot!

MODEL	Talbot Sunbeam Lotus (Type 81)
YEARS PRODUCED	1979-1981/82
BODY & CONFIGURATION	Pressed-steel unitary construction based on production Chrysler/Talbot Sunbeam front engine, rear drive hatchback. Full 4-seater with liftback luggage space.
PURPOSE	Fast road use with rally versions. Homologation special.
CHASSIS & SUSPENSION	No separate chassis. Front suspension by MacPherson strut and antisway bar. Rear suspension by solid axle and combined shock absorber and coil spring. Disc front, drum rear brakes with servo.
ENGINE	2.2-liter Lotus all-alloy 16-valve Twincam producing 150 bhp with twin Dell'Orto carburetors. Type 911.
TRANSMISSION	5-speed all-synchromesh ZF gearbox. Hypoid-bevel differential, 3.9:1 ratio. Disc front and drum rear brakes. Alloy 13-inch 6J wheels.
NOTES	Total built 2,308.

Should you come across one of these cars, beware of forgeries. Check numbers to see if a Lotus engine has been put into a similar but mundane Sunbeam 1300/1600. Look over the front suspension for distorted turret tops and suspension legs canted backward from the strain of heavy braking. As always, look for leaks around the engine and leaking or decaying fuel lines. Naturally, you should examine the entire car for rust.

It is interesting to note the clean lines of the Sunbeam Lotus—no front spoilers or rear wings. "They did nothing for the car," said Talbot's Competition Manager Des O'Dell after the car's triumph in Britain's ultratough RAC Rally.

The Mk 1 Sunbeam Lotus was finished in black with a silver side-winder incorporating a large Lotus roundel badge (all rather "boy racer" and a sure way to attract the traffic cops). It also had a pathetic six-gallon fuel tank (i.e. about 100 very fast miles range!).

On the Mk 2 version the headlamp size was increased so you could see the road ahead at 100-plus mph. The tank capacity increased by 2½ gallons. They were also finished in attractive Moonstone Blue and Silver although the original colors were still available. At the end of the production run, a firm called Avon Coachworks reputedly purchased 100 cars and custom painted them to clients' orders. Parts are still available but getting rarer by the minute.

You won't usually find a left-hand-drive Sunbeam Lotus in Britain but I am told that over 200 were sold in France. Just how an American would set about getting such a car legally imported into the United States is far from clear, as you can expect no help from Lotus, Chrysler or Peugeot France. I predict that the Sunbeam Lotus will one day become one of the "hot classic sedans" of all time and an investment to appreciate.

Talbot Sunbeam Lotus (Series 1). This is a Chrysler UK press release shot. Neat hot rod. Club Lotus England

Talbot Sunbeam and no mention of Lotus on these factory (Talbot) rally cars. Outright winner of Britain's most demanding rally, the Lombard RAC, in 1980. Note wheel arch extensions and change to a "T" from the pentastar in the front grille, but "small" headlamps.

What to look for

A Sunbeam Lotus should be road tested for at least twenty miles to ensure that all is well in every department. The ZF gearbox can misbehave when the oil is hot; some of the early engines start to lose oil pressure after about ten miles of hard driving. The brakes can be a little erratic and pull to one

Talbot Sunbeam Lotus, second series and near the end. Note headlamp and grille change and stick-on Lotus badge. Not a car you would want just anyone to valet park.

side one time and then to the other the next so use caution. Also check the silver self-adhesive side-winders, as these are almost impossible to replace and bubble up near the fuel filler cap and around the rust-prone wheel arches.

Driving impressions

Drivers of the Sunbeam Lotus should heed a simple warning in the early stages: Proceed with caution. Because Lotus had to work within the track and wheelbase limitations of the original 1300 cc Sunbeam bodyshell, the car is too short for the average-ability driver (i.e., it is very quick to snap out of shape in a turn or even under dramatically hard acceleration). In fact, the wider wheels and extra offset made the car almost square in its road-to-track ratio. To Cortina Lotus lovers this is just a Mk 3 version with more power and better brakes.

The five-speed ZF gearbox may jiggle a little in the early Lotus tradition and prove notchy to the newcomer, but the ratios are perfect and that lazy overdrive fifth is a joy for fast cruising. Like the Cortina Lotus the car and driver sit high, almost Mercedes-style, making sway seem greater than it really is.

The biggest problem with the Sunbeam Lotus is tire choice; they do need to be re-equipped with 60-series tires on bigger diameter rims such as Goodrich Comp T/A II or Goodyear NCT Eagles. In the UK, where most Sunbeams were sold, a firm called Skip Brown carried out all the factory-approved rally and Stage II High Performance modifications. It does everything from suspension to engine work.

Letting go with 6000 rpm on the tachometer will send the car forward like a rocket

The Avon Talbot Sunbeam Lotus by Avon Coachworks of Warwick. Avon bought the last 50 and customized them.

with just enough rear wheel spin to get up on the cam where all the power is. Gear changes can be made as fast as your wrist will move, and with a 6600 rpm redline the horizon is soon reached. In the wet, a great degree of caution is required in the application of full power because the car will slew sideways as you take up the drive after changing into second or even third at high revs—it is that powerful. Hitting the brakes hard in the dry means that the car stops, that's all. No nose dives or weaving—they are beautifully developed. Fast cornering is an acquired art because even with a Skip Brown Tarmac setting rear suspension, the feel of the car does not inspire the same confidence as an Elan, due to the nervous, short chassis. But once you get the hang of the handling, the car can be hustled through turns astonishingly fast.

This little tin box with over 160 bhp available up front will exceed 125 mph and amaze a lot of heavy-metal motorists in the process —but that was the Chapman tradition.

Sunbeam Lotus repainted in the original Cortina Lotus green and white livery. Club Lotus England

Lotus in the United States

Since the early sixties various importers have handled Lotus in the United States. Unfortunately, most of these commercial associations ended with acrimony and even legal actions.

In the fifties the situation had been rather turbulent with Jay Chamberlain of Lotus Cars of America importing race cars and future products. Jay was based in downtown Burbank, California. By later Lotus dealer standards he "put his money where his mouth was" for several years. He raced an Eleven with great success and seemed dedicated to the future of the marque.

In 1960 Chamberlain's impetus as the world's largest distributor of Climax Elites and Sevens, not to mention racing cars, was declining due to quality problems and ex-factory price increases. At one point, there were 100 unsold Elites in the United States.

Then the crunch came. Chamberlain was voted out of his own company by his stockholding codirectors, and Lotus transferred the franchise to Western Distributors, Inc., providing it picked up the distressed stock of cars and parts. On the East Coast, Peter Pulver and Newton B. Davis joined forces to handle Lotus from Miami to the Canadian border.

Western Distributors, Inc., faded in 1961-62 and handed over the area to Bob Challman, a Swede. He named his company after his wife Shirlee, who was tragically killed in a car accident along with his children. Ecurie Shirlee sold a lot of cars and produced a series of advertisements in *Road & Track*, many of which are collector items today.

The Midwest market was handled from 1962 on by Jim Spenser of Span, Inc., and Ed Tucker and Homer Rader handled the Texas area out of Dallas.

Unfortunately, just as the Elan became established in the United States, Challman experienced both personal and business problems relating to the death of his family. The West Coast operation went to Kjell Qvale and his massive British Motors Company.

The association prospered and when Qvale acquired Jensen cars in England it was only natural that the new Lotus engine should be fitted to the New Jensen-Healey.

When Span, Inc., stumbled due to Spenser's involvement in trying to beat Bob Tullius in a seemingly identical Triumph TR3A, Sports Cars Unlimited (which put Lotus on the scene in Canada) extended its activities into the United States. Meanwhile, Dutchess Auto continued to sell more than twelve percent of total Lotus production year after year, with a little drama and a massive parts back up.

When British Motors started to fall out of favor with Lotus over the cars, engines for Jensen and a reputed demand from British Leyland to "clean house," plans emerged for a joint company in the United States, operated by the importers. The plans were not brought to fruition, however, and for a while David Cohen, a multimillionaire Datsun dealer, gave the franchise to his son Mark, who lost interest. At this point (1978), Lotus stepped in and, with the assistance of its Canada West Coast importer as consultant, set up Lotus Cars of America, Inc., with executives shipped in from the UK.

Meanwhile, on the East Coast, Duchess Auto began consulting lawyers. The company had an automatically self-renewing contract, if it took over ten percent of Lotus production and wanted to keep the franchise or be adequately compensated. Challman sued for $1 million but was paid $200,000 in an out-of-court settlement. By this time Duchess Auto was based in Miami, with its new-car warehouse and parts operation still in New York State.

Just as amalgamation between the established importers seemed likely, Lotus made a deal with Rolls-Royce giving Rolls the entire United States distributorship. Why Rolls-Royce took this step has never been adequately explained, but the deal went sour almost as soon as the ink was dry on the paperwork. Very few cars were sold after the initial inherited stock passed into the dealer's hands. It was thought that Rolls-Royce could combine the low gas consumption of Lotus with its own gas guzzlers to avoid massive penalties. Then a minimum sales volume figure made them safe.

The arrangement was terminated in 1985 without legal action or recrimination. After a short silence as to their intentions in the United States, it was announced that Lotus Performance Cars of Norwood, New Jersey, had been formed to distribute, market and support Lotus cars in North America. It was made obvious that this new company would have the benefit of the Esprit S3 and Esprit Turbo fully certified and detoxed for the United States.

Today, the relationship is said to be "strained" between Lotus and its latest distributor in the United States (In January 1987, Lotus purchased the company). The comparison between the pound and the dollar is only just favorable to pricing and profitability, and the Lotus factory is giving 101 percent support in every way. How and if this latest setup can withstand the slings and arrows of outrageous fortunes of the US imported sports car market remains to be seen.

As most readers know, Colin Chapman, founder and guiding force behind Lotus, died of a massive heart attack on December 16, 1982, at a time when the company was at its all-time financial low. One of Britain's more dynamic motor trade entrepreneurs acquired a majority holding a few months later. After having stamped his own flair and brand of management on every aspect of the company, Lotus seems set for a whole new era of expansion and profitability, both individually and in association with Toyota of Japan.

It has been announced that General Motors has acquired Group Lotus Car Companies Limited by buying up all privately owned and corporate shareholdings, including the twenty percent stake held by Toyota of Japan. This purchase was made mainly to gain access to the enormous creativity and expertise shown by the Technology Consultancy section of Lotus.

How independent the company will remain and what will happen to the existing product range is outside the scope of this book. Lotus collectors should keep a close watch on any decision by Lotus to reduce involvement with the parts support of earlier cars, although the specialists would, in most cases, be able to pick up the problem as they have in the past. The death of Chapman, followed by the GM takeover, effectively closes the history books on Lotus as a David among Goliaths.

Restoration tips

As you can see from the overall summary of the various Lotus cars built between 1953 and the present day, they are divided into two groups: those that combine a metal chassis frame with a steel or aluminum bodyshell, and those that combine a steel chassis frame with a fiberglass bodyshell. The latter is more desirable and easier to restore, especially the "basket cases."

Earlier cars like the beautiful Eleven can still be rebodied by Williams & Pritchard, the original aluminum specialists. From the Elan S1 onward, Lotus can supply complete replacement bodyshells or sections. The famous all-fiberglass monocoque Elite (Climax) is well served by the officially appointed specialists, Fiberglass Services. Its proprietor, Miles Wilkins, is also the author

The steel-backbone chassis featured on the Elan. It was originally designed as a test bed.

of the definitive book on fiberglass restoration and repair.

Replacement chassis and body panels for the Lotus Seven are manufactured by the official factory licensee, Caterham Cars, Ltd. Alternative replacement backbone chassis on the spaceframe principle can be obtained for the Elan, Europa and Plus 2 from Spyder Limited.

I mention these firms because they have received continuous recommendation of owners, and because most are officially recognized by Lotus as approved aftermarket suppliers. There are, of course, many other restoration sources you can investigate also.

There are four things to consider before starting a restoration project:

1. Avoid a basket case; there are always more parts missing than you can imagine.

2. The job will take twice as long as you anticipate.

3. The job will cost twice as much as you budget.

4. You may need a marriage counselor before the job is finished.

On a more serious note, here is a check list I have used with success in the past. And you may find it useful.

1) Obtain all possible technical backup information from workshop manuals, reprinted service bulletins, magazine articles, road tests and so on. You cannot read enough before you start! Also join at least two Lotus clubs to get in contact with people who have done similar work on their own cars (some masochists can't wait to do it all over again).

2) Ask yourself if you really have the dedication and determination to see this project through. It is better to quit now than forever have an unfinished project.

3) If you decide to go ahead, adopt a one-thing-at-a-time approach. Work your way around the car in a logical manner, removing one section at a time. Make sure you label and store all parts accurately.

A new chassis being prepared for fitment to a Lotus Elite; the body is in the other garage. Club Lotus England

4) Keep a diary of the entire project. It adds to the value of the finished car and shows just how detailed the restoration was, especially if you really tore it down to the proverbial "last nut and bolt." Also take photographs frequently.

5) Find a workshop that you can use for a long period. It is no fun having to move a partially completed restoration from place to place.

6) Make sure the selected workshop is big enough for more than one car. Otherwise when you separate the chassis and body one will have to go outside or be hung from the rafters.

7) Make sure you have two big fire extinguishers and a fire blanket, just in case.

8) Be prepared with off-the-road restoration insurance.

9) Make out a work schedule listing tasks you can do yourself, those your unpaid volunteers (if any) can do and the jobs that will have to be financed.

10) Make a list of tools and equipment you need—what you have on hand, and what you will need to borrow, rent or steal.

Every car has its own unique quirks, and a Lotus is certainly not an exception. The following are a number of Lotus idiosyncrasies and problem areas. You should be aware of them early in your search for a particular model. Some are unique to Lotus while others are common among all cars.

Vibration

1) Aerodynamic buffeting if the windows are open.

2) Poor wheel balancing, damaged wheels or tires that are not completely round. This is especially annoying on rear wheels and can cause premature shock-absorber failure.

3) Shafts out of balance or incorrectly angled. Rebuilt cars can be fitted with badly

Rust has destroyed the strength of this early Elite chassis. Later chassis are galvanized and have a seven-year corrosion warranty. Spyder Ltd

balanced or bent shafts, or the gearbox or differential may be incorrect, thus putting the shafts through unusual angles of rotation. All can be checked at minimal cost.

4) Badly rebuilt engine—unbalanced crank, rods, flywheel and so on.

Cutout

Lotus pioneered the fitment of a cutout in the distributor. This worked via a centrifugal weight which cut off the high tension spark at optimum safe revs. A car with this unit removed or tampered with can cause quite a bit of frustration, and the warranty would be revoked by the factory.

Clutch judder

This is seldom an actual clutch problem, but rather a defect in the driveline or rear suspension area. Check the engine mountings, gearbox mountings, and tie-rods.

Air box

Most Lotus models are fitted with an airbox to provide balance around the air inlets to the carburetors. This is sometimes fed from a separate filter via flexible tubing. If the airbox has been removed the engine will draw in grit- and dust-laden air, causing premature bore wear. It also is impossible to obtain a steady, slow idle speed without a sealed box. Premature valve burring can also occur, along with fire risk on very cold mornings or at high revs. Only racing cars draw their air supply directly into the carburetors, since the engines are rebuilt every few hundred racing miles, and idle is not required.

Air cleaner

All Lotus Twincam- and 907-engined cars *must* be fitted with the correct type of air cleaner and trunking. A Lotus engine is designed to run in a "balanced depression." Therefore, open trumpets are not used, for two reasons:

1) At high revs, there is a deadly "cone" of fuel mist that actually stands out from the air intake and easily catches fire. A backfire during a cold start will also start a fire.

2) It would be almost impossible to achieve a steady idle and eliminate rough running in the middle speed range without a full air cleaner. The pancake type will not work as a substitute.

Fire

A well-known Lotus club in the United States has a Fire Secretary who keeps a record of all Lotus burnouts in an effort to discover common causes. The majority of fires are caused by faulty, loose or fractured fuel lines, and many more start electrically.

Early Lotus fuel tanks are known to rust through after a while and can cause problems. Here are some simple rules to follow:

1) Carry a *large* fire extinguisher.

Spyder chassis for Elan. M. Brown

Glassfiber accidents can happen, but always remember to pick up the pieces. Club Lotus England

Part of this is still salvageable. Club Lotus England

2) Perform regular maintenance and inspection of the fuel system and electrics.

3) If you smell gasoline or burning, stop, switch off the engine and investigate with caution.

4) Fit an inline fuel filter to remove rust particles from the fuel.

5) Fit aircraft-type fuel lines and connections.

Many Lotus fires are caused by owners during routine repairs or restoration, especially when they fail to carry out all safety checks before starting the engine. Always keep the car insured when undergoing a major rebuild or repair.

Wheel

Most Lotus cars have wheels based on the pressed-steel wheels and pitch-circle diameter of contemporary production cars. For example, the wire wheels on the top-of-the-line Mk 1 Lotus Seven came directly from MG; the pressed-steel wheels for the Elan were based on those from an Austin-Healey Sprite. On the Lotus Eleven, Lotus pioneered cast-magnesium "wobbly web" wheels which proved very easy to chip, or weakened through corrosion.

Years later, Lotus launched its own Brand Lotus knock-off wheels for the Elan Plus 2 and the later Europa Twincam Special. These were a peg-drive, center-lock unit with rims that proved to be porous, thus needing inner tubes, and they were rather susceptible to chips and cracks. The face angle for the center-lock nut was different for the alloy wheels than for the original steel wheels on the Plus 2, so new nuts have to be purchased if you need to upgrade (out of choice) or downgrade (out of necessity). These alloy wheels are now very rare, and used ones are usually in poor or unsafe condition.

The current line of Lotus cars has high-quality proprietary alloy wheels, but need a lot of care and attention to maintain the very best appearance.

Radio

Lotus never totally mastered the problems presented by fiberglass construction when it came to installing a top-quality radio. The better sound in earlier models was achieved by layering silver foil under the hood, wiring every instrument or piece of heavy metal to ground them and making sure the ignition system was heavily screened

The Lotus Elite front end is designed to absorb a lot of impact damage!

and the alternator suppressed. Despite all of this, the average Lotus sound system will always give inferior performance. However, this does not apply to stereo tape systems.

Suspension

Colin Chapman decreed that the suspension of all *road going* Lotus cars should not be adjustable. He issued this "order" because he believed, "make the suspension adjustable and they will adjust it wrong—look what they can do with a Weber carburetor in just a few moments of stupidity with a screwdriver." In fact, when the manufacturer's tolerances were very bad on early Lotus Europa models, Development Engineer Derek Sleath "sneaked in" a length adjustment and was almost sacked on the spot when Chapman saw it. The critical length was then achieved very temporarily by bending the offending rods.

Some degree of adjustment of rack height is available to the Elan and Plus 2 owners via shims. This is to adjust out excessive "bump-steer" which can occur. All genuine Lotus and Spyder replacement chassis actually have the shim thicknesses required for the rack platform inscribed on the chassis. When an alignment check is carried out that indicates some marginally incorrect figures for rear toe-in on independent suspension Lotus cars, adjustment can usually be carried out with shims (or washers). But Colin Chapman decreed that you will not be able to "dial in" handling characteristics of your choice.

Parts

Perhaps only Rolls-Royce provides as much product support via its parts department for early cars as does Lotus. It is still ninety percent possible to build a new Lotus Elan, Plus 2 or Europa through the Lotus parts catalog. And, of course, the Lotus Seven is still in production at Caterham Cars.

Lotus was affected by the same problems that have beset low-volume, specialist sports car importers in the United States during the early 1980s. There were two changes in importers, and at least seventy-five percent of the dealers gave up the franchise.

The parts support for earlier models was then taken over almost completely by specialists based in the United States or exporting directly from the United Kingdom. Some

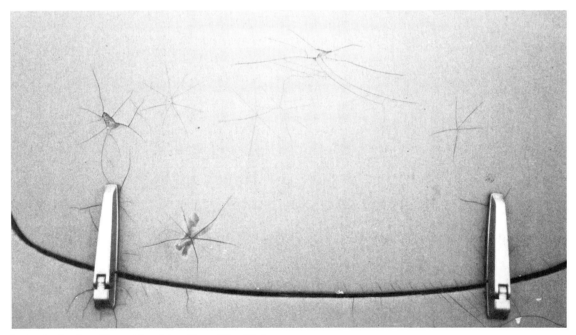

A typical glassfiber blemish, Elan S1. Club Lotus England

drew on the experience of former Lotus America executives and gave splendid service, while others based their claim to expertise on a greasy shop manual and a need to make money quickly. Therefore some research is necessary before entrusting your car or parts order to anyone outside the Lotus franchise chain.

A Lotus car is not a mixture of parts from various manufacturers' parts bins, shaken up and then poured out with a Lotus badge, but many parts are common to other makes for various reasons.

1) Common suppliers. Lotus would go to a parts supplier with specifications on a project car and ask what would fit. The supplier would then recommend a setup that might be exactly the same as on an existing car with similar demands.

2) Another manufacturer's part fitted without modification. It has been said that Colin Chapman slept with van and light-truck parts lists under his pillow. He chose these and not the equivalent car parts because they were usually cheaper. When designing a new project he would draw on his almost computerlike brain and buy components from other vehicles. These parts could be obtained from the appropriate dealers, once a hawkeyed outsider spotted the similarity.

3) Another manufacturer's part modified by Lotus. Typically, many parts fitted to a Lotus are not lifted directly from the other cars. Instead they have important and often safety-related modifications, or they are made to a higher specification.

4) Manufactured by Lotus. A very high proportion of today's Lotus cars are manufactured in-house at Hethel or from special tooling owned exclusively by Lotus. This includes engine, suspension, other alloy castings, glass and so on. These parts are often expensive but no more than other exotic, low-volume specialist imports from Europe.

Fiberglass

Most problems with Lotus fiberglass are owner related and curable, including things such as badly repaired accident damage, poorly matched paint, brake fluid and other solvent spills, and water ingress due to overzealous stripping.

From a cosmetic point of view, surface cracks and crazing look bad and take a lot of money to correct. One can't just add another coat of paint—the faults come through very quickly. In some cases a previous owner may have decided to widen the fenders to accommodate wider wheels and tires. These can be removed by a good automotive fiberglass shop. The best way to choose one of these specialists is by examining samples of their finished work. A fiberglass boat repairer is also a very good possibility.

Replacement body sections can be obtained from Lotus in England through dealers. Some very good reproductions come cheaper through US sources, although Lotus lawyers would like to stop their activities. Currently, Lotus legal teams are continuing an international campaign to restrict, where possible, the production or sale of components that are a copy of parts to which Lotus has the patent. This is being done to ensure the safety of the Lotus owner and Lotus profits.

Lotus backbone chassis

Many present (and future) cars from Chapman's stable feature an almost unique steel-backbone chassis. Ron Hickman, Lotus development director, recalls how progress on what was then supposed to be the fiberglass monocoque Elan roadster was so far behind schedule that it was impossible to

A part body section almost ready for paint on this Elan. Club Lotus England

road test the running gear. During speeches at a racing club dinner in London, he and Chapman sketched out a temporary structure based on the "fold along the dotted line" principle. Hickman's staff then made up the first backbone chassis as a mobile test rig for engine, transmission and suspension.

When an unstressed Elan bodyshell was flexibly mounted on this chassis everyone was amazed by its docility and lack of noise, harshness and vibration. This became the first pressed-steel-backbone chassis. It consisted of a deep, inverted U-section backbone with forked members branching up front to pass either side of the engine where they were joined by a front cross-member. The front suspension turrets were mounted on the cross-member, as was the vacuum tank for the pop-up headlamps.

A bridge ran across the rear of the chassis to accommodate the differential. Two outriggers held the Chapman strut rear-suspension top-mounting points with heavy rubber Lotacones. The entire structure was arc welded to very high standards of dimensional integrity by a firm called Thompsons. Later chassis would be made in-house off the same jigs.

Rustproofing consisted of an uneven application of low-quality, red leaded paint, but no rust-buildup zone was anticipated in the design except for a minute drainhole in the front suspension turrets. These became blocked quickly unless kept clear with a jiggle pin.

Since 1982 all current-range and replacement Lotus chassis are galvanized and come with a five-year anticorrosion warranty. This is rather meaningless, since the old unprotected units last, on average, eight to ten years.

Nearly ready for paint. Careful work is well worth the effort. Simon Thwaite.

When Lotus came to design the Europa, it had little faith in the backbone chassis for mid-engined cars due to the failure of the Lotus 30. The design had inherently very low torsional rigidity. (I even had a photo of Jim Clark at Riverside with the right front wheel off the ground under massive acceleration even though he was going in a straight line!) However, when the chassis was used to accommodate only 100-150 bhp, the problems went away and there was no need for outriggers.

An immediate problem with mid-engined cars, however, was sympathetic vibration. The two members passing on either side of the engine picked up vibrations from the engine mounts like a massive tuning fork. This was transferred into the firewall behind the driver and into the entire cabin structure. This made for very unpleasant, booming periods, especially when slowing on a closed throttle or even between gear shifts. No amount of sound deadening could solve the problem. It grew even worse when carried over to the Esprit.

The problem was all but eliminated in the S3 Esprit and Turbo by changing the back end to a tubular spaceframe design. The backbone concept was further developed for the Elite and Eclat (Sprint) models. Of course, Chapman later sold this inexpensive but highly effective layout to John Z. DeLorean for his DMC-12 cars.

The first known backbone-chassis car was a Tatra from behind the Iron Curtain. DeTomaso, a Chapman fan, showed a V-8-powered backbone concept at Turin in the mid-1960s. Nothing ever came of the DeTomaso design—even though Chapman was said to have had involvement in both chassis and engine.

The backbone chassis is prone to rust. Furthermore, what would probably be considered minor damage on a conventional car can derange a Lotus chassis enough to require complete replacement. It is not usually possible to straighten a bent backbone chassis or patch rusted-out areas. New, front-suspension mounting pins can be fitted after curb impact damage but requires a specialist to repair successfully. The rather simple nature of the chassis makes replacement relatively inexpensive, and the availability of a complete chassis means that a bodyshell can go on forever, as it will never rust or degrade.

If you are planning to purchase a used Lotus, for other than immediate total restoration, spend a lot of time examining the chassis. This should include probing for rust, looking carefully for cracks and then a complete alignment check. Also be sure that the car is symmetrical in all major dimensions by using the suspension pick-up locations as your reference points.

Lotus/Ford Twincam

Chapman had worked with Harry Munday, engine designer and journalist, in the early days of Coventry Climax and they respected each other's abilities. Chapman contacted Munday to work out a possible dohc version of a Ford-based engine. So the two went to work on a head design to fit a 109E three-bearing 1340 cc Ford (English) engine commonly found in the Classic/Capri. Naturally they had to use the traditional table cloth supplemented with paper napkins.

Cosworth had already extracted prodigious amounts of additional power from this engine for the Super Seven in pushrod form. Its smaller brother was the basis for the Cosworth SCA "screamer" that dominated the single-seater racing class. Chapman always had a deep respect for the high-quality, thin-wall, lightweight casting produced by Ford Dagenham, England. It was very rigid and the weight penalty, compared with aluminum, far exceeded the cost and reliability bonuses.

The Chapman/Munday layout called for a new twin overhead camshaft cylinder head cast in aluminum. Wide-angle valves were set in a hemispherical combustion chamber. The cams were driven by a chain running at the front of the engine, encased in a timing cover, that attached to the machined front face of the Ford block. The original camshaft remained as a jack shaft to operate the mechanical fuel pump. The standard Ford crank, rods and oil pump were also retained.

As the project progressed Chapman's relationship with Ford became so good that he had almost total access to Ford's future plans. This included details of the proposed new 1500 cc five-bearing crank engine. In no time, a block was procured and the Chapman cylinder head was adapted to fit. Chapman was absolutely elated, as he could see he was about to have the best 1500 cc twincam ever produced. Unlike Alfa Romeo and Fiat alternatives, this engine would both breathe and rev, yet retain a mass of torque in the right places.

How right he was! This engine was very successful right from its debut. Club Lotus claims that the Lotus/Ford Twincam has won more races than any other engine—ever. True or false, the success records go back over twenty-two years, and every weekend Lotus/Ford Twincam-engined cars notch up more and more victories.

The original 1500 cc (1498 cc) engine developed a claimed 100 bhp at 5700 rpm. When twenty-five of these engines, fitted to 1962 Elans, left the factory, Chapman made an uncharacteristic gesture and recalled all these units, replacing them free of charge, with the new, larger-capacity 1558 cc engines. Lotus decided to rationalize production at a higher capacity to enable the racing versions of the Cortina Lotus to benefit from the maximum capacity of the 1600 class. However, Lotus had a bunch of orders for racing versions of the old engines which were promptly rebuilt and placed in Lotus 23Bs.

The road-going Twincam needed and received an absolute minimum of modification and improvement from unit one to well beyond unit 40,000. Early 1558 cc units had suspect connecting rods with the ability to ventilate the cylinder block if the 6500 rpm electronic rev limiter was used as an audible means of determining the next up-shift. The C-type rod was introduced and the problem was solved. Those who wanted even more protection fitted their engines with Cosworth steels rods that were safe up to 7800 rpm. All-steel racing versions can produce up to 200 bhp.

After about 1,000 units had been produced for the Elan and Cortina Lotus, the flywheel was made more secure by going from four to six bolts. Oil pressure was always set at forty pounds at normal temperature, which was totally adequate for long engine life (100,000+ miles) with regular oil and filter changes. I recommend a top-quality 20/50 multigrade, even synthetic, oil change every 2,000 miles in winter and

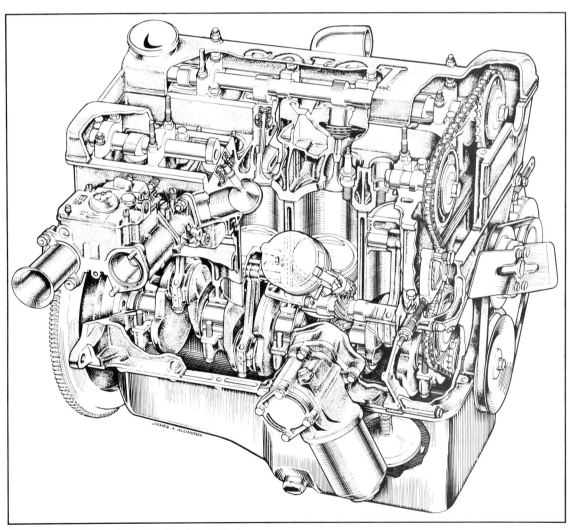

Cutaway section of the Lotus-Ford Twincam engine. James Allington and the Ford Motor Company

Vegantune's conversion to do away with the Stromberg CD carburetors on the US version of the Twincam. Replacements are by Dell'Orto.

4,000 miles in summer. The engine, however, is not happy with very thin oils.

All the models will put out a puff of smoke when the engine is started or pulled away from a stop. Clouds of smoke point to the need for a rebore or sleeves, as well as calling attention to the valve guides. Production engines don't have valve-guide oil seals but they can be retrofitted to all units except with the nonstandard high-lift cam.

The 105 bhp Twincam in the 1964 Elan and Cortina Lotus was supplemented with the Special Equipment engine, boasting 115 bhp. This engine had modified cam profiles and revised choke, jet and ignition settings. A four-bladed fan and a "hot climate" thermostat were specified for some export models. Cars for export also had 100 percent antifreeze following problems in the Midwest and Canada.

To meet US antipollution legislation, a new cylinder head was designed with differ-

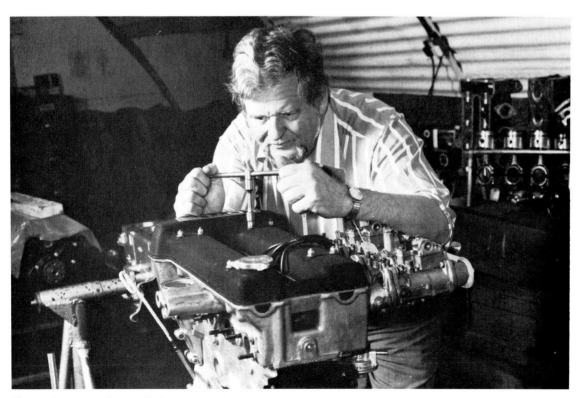

The author completes a Twincam rebuild on his own engine, at Vegantune.

ent inlet ports to accommodate twin Stromberg CD carburetors. US-market carburetors also had twin crossover pipes. Early units suffered badly from carburetor icing at high speeds and plug failures due to lack of testing. These same carburetors were fitted on the British models for a while but the company soon reverted back to twin-choke Weber or Dell'Orto. Eventually the twin Stromberg installation was debugged and, in the hands of an experienced tuner, the engine was faster and revved more freely than the seemingly more efficient Weber-equipped units. To meet stringent clean air requirements, the distributor was modified to give a greater retard on tickover. This is often mistaken for vacuum advance and retard setup.

When Tony Rudd arrived at Lotus from BRM, one of his first assignments was to extract more power from the Twincam without increasing capacity. His experience in making the best racing Twincams at BRM told him that a slight increase in the size of the inlet valve, in conjunction with new camshafts and jetting, would bring a worthwhile power bonus. This would also deliver more torque without running into tooling costs or warranty claim problems.

The engine was dubbed the Big Valve and was fitted to the Elan Plus 2 and other versions of the Seven. Beware! An engine with a crackle-finish cam cover that declares itself to be a Big Valve may not be what it seems. Some owners have removed all the paint from the cam covers and polished them to look like chrome. The only totally unfinished covers were on the Cortina Lotus and Ford Escort Twin Cam.

The true cause of Twincam water pump failure has never really been proved to be excessive sideloads from overtightening of the fan belt driving the generator or alternator—but they are a weak point in this engine. Vegantune has now developed an alternative front cover and a quick-fit capsule that can be changed in minutes. Its

The big-valve Twincam that produced around 120 bhp, not the claimed 130 bhp.

Vegantune's updating of the Lotus Twincam theme with belt drive and a lot more power using a Ford 1600 block.

147

larger bearings solve the problem, especially at sustained, high engine speeds.

This unit is famous for oil leaks but careful assembly and the frugal use of modern sealants can result in an oil-tight unit. But then the chassis rusts much quicker!

Top-end noises are a sign of tappet bucket ovality more often than camshaft wear, and noises from the engine front cover can usually be lessened via the timing chain tensioner adjusting screw. A noisy rattle denotes a loose belt and a vacuum-cleaner-type "whirr" suggests overtightening and impending camshaft failure.

Wear takes place in the usual highly stressed area such as the bores, valve guides and bearings. There is a maximum safe rebore limit of 40 thousandths; after this you will need liners.

Cylinder heads are prone to stress and fatigue cracks from the plug hole to the inlet and exhaust valves. Although not recommended by purists, skilled aluminum welding is the only solution, followed by careful remachining since these heads are no longer available from Lotus for Weber- or Dell'Orto-equipped engines. There is only a small supply of Stromberg heads remaining today. Despite rumors, there are no confirmed plans to restart production of the head.

People often claim that their Lotus has a "so and so" engine, thereby implying it is special or more valuable. Over the years the Lotus Twincam was officially race prepared for Lotus or Ford Motor Company by four well-known companies. One of them, Vegantune, is still very involved in this business, while the others, BRM, Holbay and Cos-

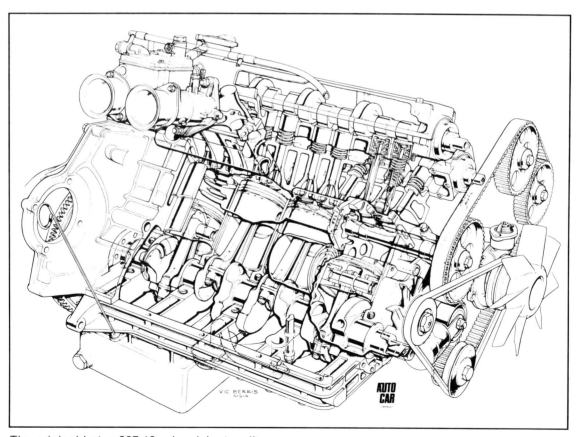

The original Lotus 907 16 valve dohc two-liter Type 907 engine in cutaway form. Business Press International Ltd worth, have all moved on to other things.

Vegantune supplied hundreds of racing twincams to Lotus, Ford and many manufacturers of Formula B single-seater race cars, like Chevron and Brabham. Its finest effort was a small batch of 1600 cc units with a genuine 200 bhp output (which were entered with Ford money in the Macau Grand Prix in the late 1960s). Today, Vegantune produces twincams from 1100 cc to almost two liters.

BRM was asked to produce modified race engines for some of the Lotus Team cars including the Mk I Cortina Lotus. The company also joined with its then number one Grand Prix driver and Lotus dealer, Mike Spence, to market a BRM modified version of the Elan. Only about ten were sold, all in BRM dark green with the distinctive Dayglo orange nose and cam cover proclaiming BRM, in green of course.

Holbay produced many very hot twincams for Formula 3 and Formula B. Presently it builds prototype engines for large manufacturers.

Finally, Cosworth was probably the best and most respected supplier of race-modified twincams or components such as cranks, cams, rods and pistons. In 1963, a set of Cosworth rods was an essential addition to any Lotus Twincam; at that time the cost was $75 per set of four. Without them the engine would be wrecked when the standard Ford rod let go at anything over 6500 rpm.

The latest 180 bhp version of the Lotus 16 valve dohc 2.2 liter engine.

The author in his road-going version of the Lotus 51 Formula Ford, beside a more serious model. Club Lotus England

Appendix

Racing road cars

Chapman went on record as saying, "No owner should be encouraged to race a street version of our cars—a total redesign is required to be competitive on any track." He was reportedly very angry when Stirling Moss, Ian Walker, Graham Warner and others started to modify Elans for racing. He was even more unhappy when some were less than successful.

Eventually, under pressure to redress the flagging reputation of his road Elan, he authorized the design and development of the 26R Racing Elan by Lotus Components Limited, under General Manager Peter Warr (now managing director of Team Lotus). As the Cortina was designed to win races from the outset, the racing versions sold by Lotus Components were not too far removed from the road cars; the rules did not permit many changes anyway, hence the initial specification.

As did the Elan, the Europa also began to appear on the track without success. So Chapman authorized the Europa type 47 with twincam power, and even obtained sponsorship from John Player for a team of cars to completely clean up in their class of British racing. After the Eleven, only the Elan, Cortina Lotus and Europa type 47 were offered ex-factory in full race trim, although a works independent rear suspension Seven was campaigned from time to time but never offered for sale.

No Elites could be purchased ex-factory specifically for racing, as this work was entrusted to David Buxton, dealer and manager of the Le Mans team. So if anyone offers you a road-based racing Lotus that has not been mentioned here, don't believe them!

From time to time, various super lightweight bodies have been supplied via the back door of the Lotus factory, in GM style, to be turned into one-off race cars. I know of several Elan, Europa, Plus 2 and Esprit shells that went that route and saw limited success in the hands of private constructors, or just disappeared.

After the Elite (Climax), Chapman dictated that Lotus road cars were *not* to be designed with racing in mind. He insisted that if, at a later date, a racing version was required, he would sit down with a clean sheet of paper and work it out. As a result the 26R Elan look-alike took sports car racing by storm, followed by the Lotus type 47 that at least looked like its Renault-powered sibling, the Europa.

No factory versions of the Eclat (Sprint), Elite or Esprit have ever been built at the factory and, as a result, their competition performances have been dismal. Some lightweight bodyshells for Esprits were made and delivered, again through the "back door," but nothing came of them either.

Earlier cars like the Elite and Eleven were extremely fragile when new. If you plan to race, consider the twenty-five years of racing, rebuilds and accidents and proceed with great caution and a lot of money. If you buy a Lotus that has been campaigned successfully for several seasons, that is a different matter—but see your bank manager and life insurance broker first. On Coventry Climax-engined cars you may run into shortages of some engine components.

Non-factory cars

Unlike many other specialist car manufacturers, Lotus never sought to have outside coachbuilders produce one-offs or limited-edition cars based on Lotus running gear. However, some specialists did manage to make contact with the factory and obtained the components required to build the following concept cars from Lotus chassis.

Frua Elan: Built by Pietro Frua in Turin to the specification of the Lotus importer for France in 1964. This car looked very much like Frua's other designs for Maserati and the Frua AC 427.

Smart Elan: These were special-bodied Elans built for Stirling Moss in 1962-63 by Williams & Pritchard and they have since disappeared. One (?) was raced successfully.

Ian Walker Elan: As with the Moss cars, these were very attractive and also built by Williams & Pritchard but with ramm tails. One is known to be in the possession of British Lotus specialist Paul Matty.

Shapecraft Elan: A very short production run of this coupe version of the S2 Elan was produced by Barry Wood of Kingston, England, in 1963-64. The first car went to actor Peter Sellers as a gift for Britt Eckland.

Elanbulance: Two such cars were built by Hexagon of London from an original Lotus concept to provide a small station wagon rear end on the Elan S3. Originally Lotus had planned to supply such a vehicle to a leading racetrack as an ambulance.

Plus 2 Convertible: Hexagon pioneered this concept of chopping the top off the Elan Plus 2. Christopher Neils of Norwich, England, has followed the concept ten years later.

GKN47D: GKN is one of the world's leading suppliers of components to the motor industry. In the mid-1960s the company asked Lotus to build a car based on the Europa type 47 GT racer, but accommodate the Buick-based Rover V-8 3.5 liter alloy engine and a five-speed ZF transaxle. One car was produced with a slightly longer wheelbase (aft of the cockpit) and is still in the hands of GKN.

Replicas, look-alikes and forgeries

There is an old Latin phrase which says *caveat emptor*, "let the buyer beware." Although somewhat nullified by modern consumer protecting legislation, the principle still applies when in the market for a used Lotus. In other words, make sure it is a genuine Lotus if you are being asked to pay *genuine* Lotus money. Some cars offered in the Lotus marketplace are acknowledged replicas, others are look-alikes or sometimes pure forgeries. Here are some examples.

Westfield: Westfield builds replicas of the Lotus Eleven and the original Mk 1 Lotus Seven. They are not 100 percent faithful to original chassis and suspension design, however; the owner may purchase an old Austin-Healey Sprite or MG Midget and put many of the parts into the Lotus replica. Chris Smith, who runs the company, fully acknowledges that these are replicas and says so on all of his documentation. They are good quality, however.

North American Sevens: When I last surveyed the world of Seven replicas I identified one firm in the United States and one in Canada. These may have been supplemented by others by now. There is also a firm claiming official Lotus recognition to make the Seven under license in South Africa. However, Graham Nearn of Caterham Cars (and his lawyers), whose company still manufactures the Seven under license from Lotus, thinks differently.

Dutton: A successful English company has produced a kit car with certain similarities (not intended I am sure) to the Seven, called the Dutton.

Costin: This car is designed by Mike Costin's brother Frank, both of whom are very respected in the sports and racing business. Mike is the "Cos" of Cosworth and Frank is the "Cos" of Marcos, the British GT car builder. Frank's latest car, built in the Seven tradition, shares certain similarities of line with the genuine Seven.

Spyder: The Spyder Silverstone is another Seven concept car built by Lotus specialist Spyder. It also builds chassis and frames as alternative fitments for some Lotus cars.

Undoubtedly there will be more to come. All the cars mentioned here, with the exception of Spyder, are honestly represented as cars with a separate identity and origin. The Spyder Silverstone is not really a lookalike at all, but an original design of considerable sophistication.

Occasionally you will run across an advertisement in the British motoring magazines for a Lotus Seven chassis and some parts. And you can be sure the chassis are forgeries, no Certificate of Origin can be obtained and, of course, the genuine Lotus chassis plate is missing. Beware!

It is also not difficult to fake a Cortina Lotus by taking a standard two-door Ford Cortina Mk 1, dropping a Lotus Twincam onto the original engine mounts, painting it white with green stripes, attaching Lotus badges and adding bumpers from a Ford van. It's not difficult to fake a Sunbeam Lotus either.

An "original" Lotus is, of course, always worth more than a customized or modified car. These modifications can be considered to alter a Lotus: wide wheel arches, wide wheels, aerodynamic devices, engines bored out more than 60 thousandths, pre-1968 engines with fuel injection, alternative engines, alternative gearboxes, "King's Road" customizing.

The Cortina Lotus and Sunbeam Lotus in rallies

In the case of both the Cortina Lotus and the Sunbeam Lotus, Lotus cars had no involvement in rally preparation or entries. In fact, the Ford and later the Talbot works cars were built from bare shells at the manufacturers' own competition facilities using nothing more than the homologation papers as a guide. "Well, so long as they look like the road cars and are legal, what the heck?" was the argument. Fuel lines went inside the bodyshell, adjustable suspensions appeared front and rear and 250 bhp engines were dropped under the hoods, at least in the Talbots. Both cars did very well due to their enormous power-to-weight ratio potential, but things move very fast in the rally world and no car stays on top of the pile for more than two years. In recent years it has taken mostly four-wheel-drive and 400 bhp to win!

There are many privately prepared rally Cortinas and Sunbeams with Lotus power, but these need careful scrutiny as they can either be "dogs" or examples of "excellent engineering." You will need to call on the services of an acknowledged local expert to help you, or ask for the list of the car's successes. A full interior rollcage, extra-wide wheel arches, extra-high-powered lights and top-quality plumbing may be your first indication that you are not looking at a normal road car.

Clubs

Joining a major Lotus club offers huge benefit and is practically invaluable. The many facilities include technical advice, access to rare parts, contact with other members with the same model, technical meets, insurance plans and access to specialists recommended by others. That alone makes joining well worth the annual dues.

Switzerland
Louis Schweiz
Unterwertstrasse 5 CH8152
Glattbrugg

Swiss Lotus Team
Postfach 57 CH3073
Gumlingen

Lotus Seven Owners Switzerland Club,
Postfach 57
CH6000 Luzern 15

Japan
Lotus Club Japan
14-3, 2 Chome, Higashi
Sibuya-ku,
Tokyo

USA
Lotus Corps
62 N Edgewood
La Grange, IL 60525

Lotus Cortina of America Register
253 Diablo Ave
Mountain View, CA 94043

Lotus Ltd.
PO Box 1
College Park, MD 20740

Lotus West Inc.
3050 Vetran Ave
Los Angeles, CA 90034

Club Elite America
23999 Box Canyon Rd
Canoga Park, CA 91304

Lotus Eleven Register
2069E Packard Highway
Charlotte, MI 48813

The Great Lakes Lotus Club
19511 Lowell
Detroit, MI 48203

Boston Area Lotus Lover Society
7 Ted Ln
Southboro, MA 01772

Golden Gate Lotus Club
40509 Ambar Pl
Fremont, CA 94538

Lotus Colorado
11050 Pyramid Pk
Littleton, CO 80127

League of Lotus Owners
8660 SE King Rd
Portland, OR 97266

Canada
Lotus Car Club of British Columbia
137 W 7th Ave
Vancouver, BC V6H-1B8

Canada Lotus Club
340 Dixon Rd
Weston, Ontario, N0B 2T0

Lotus Ontario
RR3 "The School"
Wellesley, Ontario, N0B 2T0

Sweden
Lotus Car Club of Sweden
Ekorrvagen 3, 310
40 Harplinge

Lotus Seven Club Sweden
S Appolloyagen 36B, 552
48 Jonkoping

France
Club Lotus France
La Pelouse
72160 Tuffe

South Africa
Historic Lotus Register of South Africa
PO Box 781017
Sandton 2146
Transvaal

Australia
Club Lotus Australia
40 Bellambi St
Northbridge, New South Wales

Belgium
Club Lotus Belgie
Jette-Fooz
276 Route de Wasseiges
B-5022 Cognelee

New Zealand
Club Lotus New Zealand
P.O. Box 27016
Auckland

Holland
Lotus Seven Club Nederland
Wolbrantskerkweg 4
1069 CX Amsterdam

Lotus Club Holland
Zuidzijdsedijk 19
3264 LG Nieuw Beijerland

England
Club Lotus
PO Box 8
Dereham, Norfolk NR19 1TF

Club Elite
The Coach House, The Street
Walberton, Arundel, W. Sussex

Historic Lotus racing: cars awaiting inspection.
Club Lotus England

Historic Lotus Register
Badgerswood, School Rd
Drayton, Norwich NR8 6EF

Lotus Seven Register
Seven House Town End
Caterham, Surrey CR3 5UG

Lotus Europa 47 Register
Wayside, Cotebrook nr Tarporley
Cheshire CW6 0JL

West Germany
Club Lotus Germany
Martinistrasse 16a
4690 Herne 2

Lotus Seven Club Deutschland
Postfach 111014
4000 Dusseldorf

A very rare special-bodied Elan by Shapecraft of England. The hardtop was actually bonded on. It's Brighton at the Speed Trials. Handsome Minilite wheels.

A Club Lotus exhibition display. Note the sign overhead!

Sources

Lotus has appointed the following English firms to handle the official sale and fitment of parts for the Elan and Europa:

Mick Spence Ltd.
School Green, Shinfield
Reading, Berks.

London Lotus Centre
Ballards Yard, High St
Edgware, Middx

Bell & Colvill Ltd.
Epsom Rd, West Horsley
Nr. Leatherhead, Surrey

Norfolk Motor Co.
242/245 Sprowston Rd
Norwich, Norfolk

Daytune
Coldhams Rd
Cambridge

Kelvedon Motors
Bourne Road
Spalding, Lincs

Automobile Workshops (AWS)
Lancaster Mews, off Hill Rise
Richmond Hill, Richmond, Surrey

Fiberglass Services
Charlton Saw Mills
Charlton, Singleton
Chichester, Sussex

Yarley Wood Service
1018 Yardley Wood Rd
Yardley Wood, Birmingham

The following is a list of English and US Lotus specialists who are independent of the factory. Although they have all been known to Club Lotus for many years you should take the usual commercial precautions before sending off large sums of money. (These codes are used to indicate the specialties of each: Eg, engine; Fb, fiberglass; Rs, restoration; Ps, parts; Ts, transmission; UL, used Lotus; Sv, service; Pt, paint specialist.)

Twincam Techniques
7 Hinckley Business Park
Dodwells Bridge Industrial Estate
Hinckley, Leics.
(Eg)

Eagle Racing
Noons Farm, Charthill Road
Chart Sutton, nr Maidstone, Kent
(Eg, Fb, Rs, UL, Pt)

Skip Brown
Ridley Green
nr Tarporley, Cheshire.
(Sunbeam Lotus specialists and 907 engine)

Crewkerne Tire Co
North Street Trading Estate
Crewkerne, Somerset
(Cortina Lotus body parts specialists)

Paul Matty Sports Cars
12 Old Birmingham Rd
Bromsgrove, Worcs.
(Rs, Ps, UL, Pt)

C. J. Foulds Motors
Commercial Mill, Frith St
Huddersfield, W Yorks.
(Rs, Ps, Sv, Pt)

Barry Ely Motors
453 High Rd
Leyton, London SW10
(Sv)

Len Street Ltd.
Drayton Gardens
London SW10
(Ps, UL, Sv)

Spyder Ltd.
Station Road Industrial Estate
Whittlesey, Cambs.
(alternative chassis specialists, Ps)

Nicol Transmissions
Coppice Trading Estate, Stourport Road
Kidderminister, Worcs. (Ts)

Morland Jones
226/227 Trussley Rd
London W4
(Sv)

Dave Gallup Carcare
Unit 1, Ironmould Lane
Brislington, Bristol
(Sv, Pt, Ps)

Robin Alabaster
Halfway Garage, Bath Road
Parworth, Berks.
(Rs, Fb, Pt)

Climax Engine Services
82 Northwick Park Estate
Blockley, Glos.
(Climax engine specialist)

E. M. Winter
9 Witham Close
Bedford
(Eg)

Norvic Engines
Westgate Hangar, The Airfield
Little Staughton, Beds.
(Eg)

Vulcan Engineering Ltd.
185 Uxbridge Road
London W7
(Eg)

Vegantune Ltd.
Cradge Bank
Spalding, Lincs
(Eg, Rs, Fb, Pt)

Terry Carthy
4E Pepper Rd, Hazel Grove
Stockport, Cheshire
(Sv)

Quorn Engine Development
Soar Rd
Quorn, Leics.
(Eg)

Christopher Neil Sportscars
Middlewich Road Northwich
Cheshire
(Eg, Rs, Fb, Ps, UL, Sv, Pt)

Midas Metalcraft
Unit 41
The Airfield, Little Staughton,
Beds.
(tubular chassis specialists 6, 7 Formula Ford)

Chris Smith (Westfield)
5 Gibbons Industrial Park
Dudley Rd, Kingswinford
W. Midlands
(Rs, emphasis on tubular chassis in Six, Seven and Eleven)

Williams & Pritchard
25 First Ave
Edmonton, London N.18
(aluminum bodies for early Lotus such as Eleven)

Lenham Motor Co
47 West St
Harrietsham, nr. Maidstone, Kent.
(hardtops for Elan)

M. Fincham Fiberglass
Boss Motors, Snetterton
Norwich, Norfolk
(body panels)

Lotus Workshop
Grindleton Ln
Ambler, PA 19002

RRS Engineering
13 Oregon St
El Segundo, CA 90245

New England Classics
50 Embree St
Stratford, CT 06497
(Parts, restorations, modifications)

Dave Bean Engineering Inc.
925 Punta Gorda St
P.O. Box 4070
Santa Barbara, CA 93103
(parts)

The Lotus factory Publications Department supplies workshop manuals and very comprehensive parts lists for the following:
Lotus Elan S1, S2, S3, S4, Sprint
Lotus Elan Plus 2, Plus 2S, Plus 2S/130 and 5-speed
Lotus Europa S1 and S2 (Renault)
Lotus Europa Twincam and Special
Lotus Elite and Eclat (Sprint)
Lotus Esprit S1, S2 and 2.2
Lotus Esprit S3 with optional turbo supplement

Order from your dealer or directly from a dealer in the United Kingdom. Cost is approximately $60.

Caterham Cars Limited can supply manuals and parts lists for the Lotus Seven and the Caterham Seven.

Fiberglass Services can help with technical advice on the Elite (Climax).

Peter Brand at the Lotus factory maintains his own personal records of the early cars built at Hornsey and Cheshunt in the 1950s and 1960s. He may be able to help (he does this for the love of the marque, not as part of his job as a quality engineer).